Sarah Kane's
Blasted

Continuum Modern Theatre Guides

Helen Iball

Sarah Kane's
Blasted

continuum

Continuum International Publishing Group
The Tower Building, 11 York Road, London SE1 7NX
80 Maiden Lane, Suite 704, New York NY 10038

www.continuumbooks.com

© Helen Iball 2008

First published 2008

British Library Cataloguing-in-Publication Data
A catalogue record for this book is available from the British Library.

ISBN: 978-0-8264-9204-3 (hardback)
      978-0-8264-9203-6 (paperback)

Library of Congress Cataloguing-in-Publication Data
A catalog record for the record for this book is available from the Library of Congress

Typeset by Newgen Imaging Systems Pvt Ltd, Chennai, India
Printed and bound in Great Britain by Cromwell Press Ltd,
Trowbridge, Wiltshire

Contents

Acknowledgements

The productions of *Blasted* staged in the UK while I was preparing this manuscript added hugely to my experience and understanding of the play in performance. Thank you to Graeae and to the Schaubühne Theatre. Particular thanks go to the directors and actors involved in these productions who were to become my interviewees: Alex Bulmer, Thomas Ostermeier, Jenny Sealey and David Toole. Their insightful and generous contributions underpin the production history chapter, while a number of sections in the workshop chapter draw upon Graeae exercises. I had these exercises described to me by Alex Bulmer and Jenny Sealey, and then was fortunate to observe a workshop at the University of Hull led by Gerard McDermott and David Toole. Thank you also to the Press Office at Glasgow Citizens Theatre for photographs and reviews of Kenny Miller's production, and to Anthony Shrubshall for the interview, photographs and workshop exercises in relation to the Questors production.

This book is a testament to all the students with whom I have explored *Blasted* over the past ten years, first at Scarborough and then at Hull. My interest in the play is rooted in my doctoral study with David Ian Rabey, whose theatrical perspectives have inspired me and whose friendship I value greatly. A very big thank you to Graham Saunders and Aleks Sierz for their generosity – this book has benefited enormously from their knowledge and support, and from access to their archives. Further thanks are due to Graham in his role as editor and to Anna Sandeman and Colleen Coalter, my publishers at Continuum, for pulling out the stops. Heartfelt thanks go to Monica Pearl for facilitate meticulous proof reading.

All quotations from Sarah Kane's *Blasted* appear with kind permission from A. & C. Black and Methuen. Extracts from *Among the Thugs* by Bill Buford, published by Secker & Warburg/Arrow are reprinted by permission of The Random House Group Ltd. Extracts from *British Society Since 1945* by Arthur Marwick (Copyright (c) Estate of Arthur Marwick) by permission of PFD (www.pfd.co.uk) on behalf of the Estate of Arthur Marwick. Quotations from Sellar, T, 'Truth and Dare: Sarah Kane's Blasted,' in *Theater*, 27 (1), 29–34, Copyright 1996, Yale School of Drama/ Yale Repertory Theatre are used with permission of the publisher, Duke University Press.

And, to Jack Alexander Head, a sentence that you will tell me should not begin with 'and'. Thank you.

Helen Iball
Leeds, December 2007

General Preface

Continuum Modern Theatre Guides

Volumes in the series Continuum Modern Theatre Guides offer concise and informed introductions to the key plays of modern times. Each book takes a close look at one particular play's dramaturgical qualities and then at its various theatrical manifestations. The books are carefully structured to offer a systematic study of the play in its biographical, historical, social and political context, followed by an in-depth study of the text and a chapter which outlines the work's production history, examining both the original productions of the play and subsequent major stage interpretations. Where relevant, screen adaptations will also be analyzed. There then follows a chapter dedicated to workshopping the play, based on suggested group exercises. Also included are a timeline and suggestions for further reading.

Each book covers:
- Background and context
- Analysis of the play
- Production history
- Workshopping exercises

The aim is to provide accessible introductions to modern plays for students in both Theatre/Performance Studies and English, as well as for informed general readers. The series includes up-to-date coverage of a broad range of key plays, with summaries of important critical approaches and the intellectual debates that have illuminated the meaning of the work and made a significant contribution to our broader cultural life. They will enable readers to develop their understanding of playwrights and theatre-makers, as well as inspire them to broaden their studies.

The Editors:
Steve Barfield, Janelle Reinelt,
Graham Saunders and Aleks Sierz

March 2008

1   Background and Context

Introduction

This chapter is an introduction to the study of Sarah Kane's *Blasted*. It explains why the play is important, gives a sketch of its author's life and discusses the social, economic and political background to the play.

Blasted opened at the Royal Court Theatre Upstairs, London, on 12 January 1995 directed by James Macdonald with Pip Donaghy as Ian, Kate Ashfield as Cate and Dermot Kerrigan as the Soldier. The play begins as forty-five-year-old Ian and twenty-one-year-old Cate meet in a hotel some years after their relationship has ended. Ian makes various attempts to cajole and then, it is implied, to force Cate to have sex with him. A bomb goes off and destroys part of the room. Ian becomes the victim as a Soldier re-enacts war crimes perpetrated on his girlfriend, who was subsequently killed. The Soldier shoots himself. Blinded, hungry and alone, Ian makes a series of desperate attempt to find relief. Cate has left the hotel in search of food and, as the play ends, returns with provisions that she shares with a finally grateful Ian. A handful of scandalized newspaper reviews – the most famous being the headline, 'This Disgusting Feast of Filth', that accompanied Jack Tinker's review of the play – were picked up by the British broadcast media, creating one of those rare occasions when theatre makes the headlines. The impact of this initial explosion of publicity has had an enduring effect. Indeed, the controversy that the play attracted, coupled with Sarah Kane's suicide in February 1999, has often overshadowed the play itself.

So it is that Mythology surrounds both *Blasted* and its author. Kane was a 1990s landmark dramatist, over-rated interloper, honorary lad, confrontational bad girl, funny, depressive, tortured suicidal artist, theatrical visionary, saviour and prophet, depending upon whom you asked and when you asked them. Such was her notoriety that the director Thomas Ostermeier recalls 'when she first came to Berlin we expected to meet an aggressive punk but found her charming and funny' (Billington, 2005). When assessing the play's importance, a parallel can be drawn with Ostermeier's preconceptions about Kane: while by reputation *Blasted* is predominantly gruesome and violent, it is also often funny and was, according to Kane, motivated by 'hope' (Kane, 1999b).

In a letter of support to the *Guardian* newspaper at the time the premiere of *Blasted* was being castigated, fellow playwrights declared: 'she dares to range beyond personal experience and brings the wars that rage at such a convenient distance from this island right into its heart' (Crimp et al., 1995). Indeed, Kane's creative impulse was ignited by the recognition that although for those in comfortable British lifestyles in the mid-1990s, civil war bursting into a Leeds hotel room seemed inconceivable, in fact, the wall between 'peacetime civilization' and the 'chaotic violence' of war was 'paper-thin'. Responding to a British media, whom she claimed wished 'to deny that what happened in Central Europe has anything to do with us' because 'they don't want us to be aware of the extent of the social sickness we're suffering from' (Stephenson and Langridge, 1997: 131), Kane literally blasted the dramatic conventions with which the contemporary audience was so comfortable. As Kane observed, the play's form is a crucial consideration because it is 'a direct parallel to the truth of the war it portrays' (Stephenson and Langridge, 1997: 130). In the bomb blast that rips apart the convention of the box-set hotel room, *Blasted* also explodes the central tenets of realist form: the representation of a 'slice of life' through a logical connection between characters and action which culminates in resolution – all of which allow the audience to remain at a comfortable distance, its existing opinions reaffirmed. In *Blasted* 'no authorial voice is leading us to safety' (Kane, 2001: ix) and this seems to be what contributed most to the outraged reactions from some members of the press.

Certainly, if the focus is only on content, *Blasted* becomes a list of atrocities – and the journalists writing those first reviews favoured lists: the play contains anal rape, frottage, urination and defecation, baby eating, cunnilingus, fellatio, the sucking and chewing of eyeballs. Yet, of course, theatrical representation usually acknowledges the limits imposed by a respect for human rights and decency. Thus, while 'the press was screaming about cannibalism live on stage' in fact these were not 'actual atrocities' but 'an imaginative response to them in an odd theatrical form' (Stephenson and Langridge, 1997: 131). As Kane observed, Ian is 'clearly not eating the baby. It's absolutely fucking obvious. This is a theatrical image. He's not doing it at all', and thus she asserts that 'in a way' such representation is 'more demanding because it throws you back on your own imagination' (Saunders, 2002: 66).

Rebecca Schneider labels scenarios in which 'viewers have to suspend their belief in order to look at some of the nasty underpinnings propping those belief systems' as 'counter-mimetic' (1997: 100) – by which she means that, 'in an almost complete inversion of naturalism, disbelief rather than belief is put forward like a dare' as the material is shoved 'squarely in your face' (1997: 101). It is, indeed, the conceptualization of 'in-yer-face' theatre that has contributed significantly to the landmark status of *Blasted*. 'In-yer-face' is the banner under which Aleks Sierz drew together a group of young British dramatists in the mid-1990s working to create what he describes as a 'compelling new aesthetic of experiential drama' (2001a: 239), using brutal and explicit techniques as a means to disrupt audience complacency. With variations across various commentators, and with alternative collective labels such as

'New Brutalists', 'smack and sodomy plays' (Clapp, 1998), 'theatre of urban ennui' (Nightingale, 1998), the featured dramatists generally include Jez Butterworth, David Eldridge, Nick Grosso, Sarah Kane, Martin McDonagh, Joe Penhall, Rebecca Prichard, Mark Ravenhill, Judy Upton and Michael Wynne. Sierz (2001a) identifies their precursors as Phyllis Nagy, Anthony Neilson and Philip Ridley.

Kane wanted to put 'the audience through the experience' of theatre and she sought to emulate the intense engagement of football and pop concert crowds (Sierz, 2001a: 98). The atrocities in *Blasted* exploit what Stanton B. Garner has labelled 'neuromimetic transferral': defined as 'the impulse to close one's eyes during simulated blindings on-stage' which 'reflects not simply an aversion to the representation of pain, but also a deeper defence against its sympathetic arising in the field of one's own body' (1994: 180–1). To demand belief in situations that exceed the realms of most people's lived experience, Kane uses powerful theatrical images, many of which have invasive visceral qualities that provoke a felt reaction. In each production of *Blasted* that I have seen, the moment when Ian 'eats the baby' (5: 60) has been staged with different levels of realism. In every instance, I have watched as a number of audience members grimace and recoil or even cover their eyes.

In *Blasted,* the neuromimetic and counter-mimetic work in combination to demand an active engagement from the audience – the reactions are to performed terrors and the repulsion implicates us because we are so accustomed to distancing ourselves from brutality. Kane tears apart the domestication of mimesis, the 'kitchen sink' realism that has been perceived as the dominant dramatic mode of the Royal Court Theatre in the post-war period. One of the most notable aspects of *Blasted* is the way in which its opening scenes accord with realist strategy while, at the same time, enclosing the seeds of other theatrical forms that dislocate the conventional unities of time, space and action, as later sections of this book explore. Mel Kenyon, Kane's agent, believes that it is 'raw emotion' in combination with 'theatrical experimentation' that distinguishes her plays (2006).

The importance granted to *Blasted* resides in its imaginative leap – it is an audacious play, in which Kane makes the very deliberate decision to express things that are far from her lived experience – yet she begins by staging an encounter that seems to draw upon a world with which she was more familiar, as this chapter goes on to consider.

About the play's author

Sarah Kane was born in Essex on 3 February 1971. Her father was a journalist with the British tabloid press. Her mother had left journalism when Kane's older brother Simon was born. Kane described how she 'hated school until the Sixth Form' (Kane 1999b) when she was inspired by English and drama. She was also a member of the Basildon Youth Theatre. Thus it was that she chose to read Drama at Bristol University. The playwright David Greig has spoken in wry tones of the intensity of his and Sarah's younger selves who were 'part of an intimate circle of gothic miserablists' at Bristol, who 'listened to Joy Division, dressed in black, raged against the slaughter in the Balkans' (Hattenstone, 2000). During her undergraduate years, Kane shifted from her interest in acting to an interest in directing and then turned to writing. It was during her studies at Bristol (1989–92) that she wrote the trilogy of monologues (*Comic Monologue*, *Starved* and *What She Said*) collectively titled *Sick*. The playwright donated copies of these scripts to the University's Theatre Collection. Kane performed the monologues on the Edinburgh Festival Fringe in 1991 and 1992.

After graduating from Bristol with First Class Honours, Kane began an MA in Creative Writing at Birmingham University. Though she was not pleased with the course, it did enable her work to be seen by theatrical agents. It was here that an early draft of the first half of *Blasted* was staged in July 1993, which Kane thought was 'really well directed' (Kane, 1998b) by Pete Wynne-Wilson. The performance was attended by Mel Kenyon of the agency Casarotto-Ramsey who became Kane's agent. In January 1994, a rehearsed reading of *Blasted* was presented by the Royal Court, directed by James Macdonald, who would go on to form a close working relationship with Kane and to direct the play's premiere (1995) and the Sarah Kane season productions (2001).

Kane moved from Birmingham to London for a job at the Bush Theatre in 1994. She had twice applied for the role of assistant director there. The theatre's Artistic Director, Dominic Dromgoole, and his team liked Kane's passion and intelligence but felt that she was probably 'too intense' for the role for which she had applied, so they created the position of literary associate for her – a job from which she was to walk out (see Dromgoole, 2000: 161–2). In autumn 1996, Kane joined Paines Plough, a company that champions new writing for theatre, as their Writer-in-Residence. Also in 1996, she directed the premiere of her play *Phaedra's Love* at London's Gate Theatre. Kane went on to direct Georg Büchner's *Woyzeck* (1879) at the Gate in 1997. In addition to writing for theatre, Kane scripted a short film, *Skin*, that was televised by Channel 4. The film was directed by Kane's close friend Vincent O'Connell, and screened in a late night slot (17 June 1997). The central character, Billy, was played by Ewen Bremner, well known for his screen performance as Spud in Danny Boyle's 1996 film of Irvine Welsh's disturbing and brutal drug-culture novel *Trainspotting* (1993).

In an unexpected turn of events, Kane took over the role of Grace in her play *Cleansed* (Royal Court, 1998) after Suzan Sylvester injured herself during a performance. In the same year that *Cleansed* opened in London, *Crave* premiered at the Traverse Theatre in Edinburgh. The play had been drafted during workshops with

Paines Plough, with Kane choosing to present her script under the pseudonym Marie Kelvedon – partly as a means to sidestep the pressures to innovate that went hand in hand with the recognition and, indeed criticism, stemming from *Blasted*. In *Crave,* the four voices do not have names, but rather are designated the letters A, B, C and M. As in *Blasted*, there is a dominant focus upon inter-generational relationships, and both plays explore complex experiences of love and desire.

Kane suffered from depression, and the bouts became increasingly severe. *4.48 Psychosis*, based on her experiences of the condition and its treatments, was produced posthumously at the Royal Court in 2000. Mel Kenyon admits 'I pretend that [*4.48 Psychosis*] isn't a suicide note but it is. It is both a suicide note and something much greater than that' (Urban, 2001: 65). In his preface to Kane's *Complete Plays* (2001) David Greig identifies the increasing insularity and personal-confessional aspects to his friend's work, suggesting this means that we, as audiences, have the opportunity to 'freight the plays with our own presence, our own fears of the self-destructive act and our own impulses towards it' (xviii).

This quality is, in fact, cyclical if the scripts preceding *Blasted* are taken into account. The preoccupations apparent in Kane's early monologues also permeate her later work, and the confessional form is one to which she returned in her last plays, *Crave* and *4.48 Psychosis*. A persistent theme throughout the canon is a young woman struggling against confining expectations and with the complexities of her identity and social interactions in terms of self-esteem, body image and eating disorders, and sexual politics – which, in part, may be related to a particular socio-historical context. It is a theme that is encapsulated in the overarching title of the monologues: *Sick*. These monologues, each with its speaker named simply 'Woman', express connections between the compulsion to purge her body of sperm after an abusive sexual encounter in *Comic Monologue* and the subsequent focus in *Starved* on bulimia, anorexia and hospitalization as an attempt at treatment. As a whole, the monologues present an overwhelming sense of a young woman growing up and facing the pressures of British society in the 1980s; Andrea Dunbar's *Rita, Sue and Bob Too* (1982) has a similar underlying dynamic. There was an imperative to flirt but accept the consequences and avoid the label 'slut', not to be a 'prick tease', but also to remember 'the woman's right to say no'. The press was preoccupied with date rape, scares about the safety of the contraceptive pill and about the risk of infection. In the mid-late 1980s HIV and AIDS were at the core of anxieties about sexual promiscuity. To be a young woman at this time was also to be implicated by media coverage of diet and body image, and of contested territory between sexual activity and feminist ideology; Kane explores the latter very vividly in her third monologue *What She Said*.

Recognizing that Kane's writing is cyclical is also to acknowledge a symbiosis between the personal and political from the outset – and have the opportunity to make this connection in a manner that grants the writer agency, her choice of suicide dignity and those encountering her work insights. Kane had her own tragic artistic icon in Ian Curtis, the lyricist and suicide lead singer of Joy Division, and thus 'would have had some sympathy with this fascination' as it 'became obvious that her life and work were being processed into the great Romantic legend of the tortured suicidal artist' (Ravenhill, 2006).

The social, economic and political context

Blasted can be understood in the context of four key areas:

1   Civil war in the Balkans during the 1990s.
2   Hooliganism. Home-grown violence 1980s–1995 (i.e. from Kane's formative years to the play's premiere).

1 Civil war in the Balkans during the 1990s

In 1993, Kane was in the process of writing what was then 'a play about two people in a room' when she saw an item about the siege of Srebrenica on the television news. Kane began searching for connections between rape in a Leeds hotel and the Bosnian civil war. 'Suddenly the penny dropped' that 'one is the seed and the other is the tree. I do think that the seeds of full-scale war can always be found in peace-time civilisation' (Saunders, 2002: 39). Steve Waters suggests that in the 1990s Britain was very much a spectator upon war and terrorism – which were perceived to happen elsewhere, being beamed into British homes by the television news:

> The dominant mode of violence in the 1990s was in fact internecine war – conflicts in the former Yugoslavia, inter-ethnic conflicts in the former Soviet Union, the first invasion of Chechnya and the horror of the Rwandan genocide. Violence, for the West at least, was elsewhere, done to others by others. (Waters, 2006: 373)

A major conflict of the 1990s was civil war in the former Yugoslavia, and it was news footage of this conflict to which *Blasted* responded. When Mikhail Gorbachev came to power in the USSR (1985) he sought to end the Cold War with the West, including unilateral agreements on arms cuts and nuclear defence. The fall of the Berlin Wall (1989) and the reunification of Germany (1990) were significant in ending divisions that had dominated post-war European history. The transition period was difficult, and the overthrow of Communism created opportunities for nationalism. There were wars in the republics of Slovenia and Croatia after the State of Yugoslavia began to break up in 1991. In April 1992, Bosnian Serbs refused to accept the Bosnian declaration of independence and to live under Muslim rule. The Serbs then launched a military offensive, which by the end of the year had been hugely effective in the aim of creating their own Bosnian Serb republic by means of ethnic cleansing, such as driving Muslim civilians from their homes. Bosnian Croats then launched a similar offensive, and the war became three-way.

Kane responded to the Serbian attacks on the Bosnian city of Srebrenica in 1993 by changing the shape of the play she was writing. These attacks led to the United Nations Security Council declaring the city one of six 'safe areas'. Two years later, in July 1995, Serbian troops overran the city, NATO air strikes having failed to stop their advance. In seeking material to express the horrors of civil war, Kane looked not only to press reports about war rape and acts of torture in the Balkans, but also to equivalents in British culture – once again, iterating the 'seed and tree' scenario by drawing parallels that brought the apparently (and comfortably) distant violence very close to British experience.

2 Hooliganism

In the action of the Soldier sucking out and biting off Ian's eyes, Kane germinated a seed that had lodged in her mind from reading Bill Buford's *Among the Thugs* (1991). Buford, an American journalist, had joined a gang of English football hooligans during the mid-late 1980s. The episode is described in the book as follows:

> He grabbed the policeman by his ears, lifted his head up to his own face and sucked on one of the policeman's eyes, lifting it out of the socket until he felt it pop behind his teeth. Then he bit it off. Harry rolled off the policeman, stood up and walked home. (Buford, 1991: 241)

Rampaging fans committing violent and criminal acts on match days, both in the UK and at away games in Europe, was a regular occurrence in the mid-late 1980s. The worst of these happened before the Liverpool v. Juventus match at Heysal Stadium in Brussels (1984) when thirty-nine people died and six hundred were injured. The running battles on the city streets of Europe were not far removed from war, with the authorities bringing in tanks and armed escorts on some occasions. Indeed, Buford later compares the hooliganism he has witnessed with a photograph of crowd behaviour in war-torn Yugoslavia (1991: 187).

For some, 1980s football violence had provided a site for the expression of extreme right-wing politics, its perpetrators declaring allegiance to organizations such as the National Front. This white supremacist attitude was expressed through factions of the skinhead subculture, which had emerged in late 1960s Britain and produced offshoots in the punk and neo-punk movements of the late 1970s-early 1980s. Skinheads had a distinctive dress code and signature shaved hair. That viewers would undoubtedly recognize these codes enables the succinct visual impact of Kane's short screenplay *Skin* (1997). The central character, Billy Boy, provides a useful point of contact between recurring themes within Kane's plays, and with specific contexts that are implied elsewhere in her writing. Acknowledgement of the tribalism of punks, skinheads and football hooliganism can add particularity to a more generalized 'laddism' and the so-called crisis in masculinity seen as symptomatic of the era:

> [A]bloated code of maleness, an exaggerated embarrassing patriotism, a violent nationalism, an array of bankrupt antisocial habits. This bored, empty, decadent generation consists of nothing more than it appears to be. It is a lad culture without mystery, so deadened that it uses violence to wake itself up.

It pricks itself so that it has feeling, burns its flesh so that it has smell. (Buford, 1991: 265)

Kane's friend Vincent O'Connell, who directed *Skin* and script-edited *Blasted*, also wrote the screenplay for the film *I.D.* (1995), which is about football hooliganism. In *Blasted*, Ian's prejudice that characterizes all football supporters as hooligans is particularly vociferous. He clearly does not recognize aspects of their violence and bigotry within himself. Furthermore, Kane uses football fan Cate to question his blanket application of the stereotype (1: 19–20), which, as Cate's bemusement implies, was by this point somewhat outdated partly as a result of tough legislation to the extent that 'by 1990 the climate had shifted from thug culture' (Buford, 1991: 270). Indeed, England hosting the Euro '96 football tournament was adopted as a symbol of the New Britain heralded by New Labour.

3 In-yer-face and the BritPack

All of Kane's plays were written and premiered over a period of less than a decade. Literally, she was a 1990s playwright. She became the reluctant figurehead of 'in-yer-face', as *Blasted* was singled out 'as a catalyst in restoring the fortunes of writing to the British stage' (Saunders, 2002: 4). A rapid assimilation into the lineage, John Osborne's *Look Back in Anger* (1956), Edward Bond's *Saved* (1965), Sarah Kane's *Blasted* (1995), provided a convenient means of according landmark status. The critic Tom Sellar comments thus:

Like John Osborne unleashing his belligerent Jimmy Porter onto the post-war British stage, Sarah Kane brings an explosive reality into our theatre that the larger culture would rather deny. Just as Osborne tapped into an angry national psyche of class resentment in the 1950s – and as Edward Bond made fierce characters and language speak for poverty and cruelty in the 1960s and 70s – Kane ventures into extremity, terror and social decay in the late 1990s. (1996: 29)

This lineage also served to locate Kane within the Royal Court's tradition of 'angry young men'. Elaine Aston observes 'apparently women are not supposed to write such violent plays' (2003: 79). One of the ways of dealing with Kane's youth and her gender was to accord her status as an honorary male – a status that was consolidated further by the laddish identity of the so-called BritPack.

While the theatre director Dominic Dromgoole asserted that 1990s drama was 'richer in total than the in-yer-face plays that formed the noisiest part of it' (Eldridge, 2003: 56), the mid-late 1990s saw the theatre reinvigorated by the noise. This renaissance can be paralleled with the rise of BritPack artists such as Tracey Emin, Sarah Lucas and Damien Hirst. Their impact is encapsulated by the aptly named Sensation exhibition at the Saatchi Gallery (London, 1997). It is no coincidence that the birth of 'in-yer-face', which tends to be identified with Judy Upton's *Ashes and Sand* (December 1994), coincides with the 1994 election of Tony Blair to the leadership of the Labour Party. This election was a sign of shift in a climate hungry for change, the Party running for government under the banner 'New Labour New Britain', and seeking out young artists to package this sentiment known as 'Cool Britannia'. Neither does it seem coincidental that Blair won the General Election in 1997, the year that some see as marking the end of 'in-yer-face', although there is equally an argument from commentators including Aleks Sierz and Ken Urban that 1997 represents its zenith. The playwright David Eldridge favours the former perspective, locating Conor McPherson's play *The Weir* (1998), and the mocking of in-yer-face by Ben Elton's novel *Blast from the Past*

(1998) in which one of the characters goes 'to see a play called *Fucking and Fucking* at the Royal Court', as 'signalling a change in direction' (2003: 55).

4 Thatcher's children

Though the 1990s context is important in understanding the particular climate in which *Blasted* was produced and received, as the recognition of 1980s football hooliganism has begun to evidence, it is equally important to consider the formative influence of the 1970s and 1980s in shaping the experience and world view of Kane and her peers: the generation dubbed 'Thatcher's children'. Margaret Thatcher became Conservative Prime Minister in 1979 and remained in that position until her resignation in 1990. Before the elections, economic recession had culminated in the 1978–9 'Winter of Discontent', with nationwide pay strikes by public service workers causing severe disruption including power cuts and piles of uncollected refuse in the streets. The Thatcher government curbed the power of the trade unions, and the encouragement of a free market economy resulted in the 1980s economic boom for Britain.

However, by the end of the decade, encapsulated in the replacement of Margaret Thatcher by John Major, confidence was floundering and by 1992 the government were forced to devalue sterling after the Stock Market collapse of 'Black Wednesday'. This concentration on individualist policy came to be encapsulated in the public consciousness by Margaret Thatcher's assertion that 'there's no such thing as society' – a statement lifted in isolation from an interview with the magazine *Woman's Own* (31 October 1987). The mid-1980s through the early-1990s were years of direct action: of IRA terrorist attacks, regional race riots (including in Leeds, the setting of Kane's *Blasted*), protests against the Poll Tax – which replaced rate charges based on property value with a community charge based on the number of household occupants – against job losses in the print trade at Wapping and against amendments to the Criminal Justice Bill. Protest marches that began with a carnival spirit all too often descended into violent clashes with the police.

Some of the most disturbing and enduring images for those, like Kane, growing up in this period, were of the 1984–5 Coal Miners' Strike, in which police – deployed for the first time in riot gear – battled with the pickets. 'The worst abuse on the police side was the repeated indiscriminate use of truncheoning' and 'even more open to criticism was the way in which mounted police were deployed'; however, at Orgrave colliery, 'it was clear that when the four mounted police were sent in to charge the crowd, police had undergone a long spell of stone throwing' (Marwick, 2003: 285). One event that resonates for *Blasted*, and that acts as a reminder that terrorism was not so unknown on UK soil as some of the early press reviews would have us believe, is the 1984 IRA bombing of the Grand Hotel, Brighton. This was an attempt to blow up Margaret Thatcher and her Cabinet during the Conservative Party Conference.

The generational experience of growing up in 1970s/1980s Britain as 'Thatcher's children' is often cited as a strong influence upon 1990s art. In essence this is characterized by the perception that community spirit had been lost, and that Thatcherite attitudes lay at the root of this loss which bred hopelessness and cynicism, as well as ignited pockets of activism. The dramatist Mark Ravenhill contemplates the notion of an 'emotional starting point' for his writing in the 1993 murder of two-year-old Jamie Bulger by two ten-year-old boys: 'there was a sort of public grief projected onto that case – grief and guilt for the decade that had passed. For the greed and neediness, the divisiveness, for the communities con-signed to the underclass' (2004: 309). Press reports focused on the number of passers-by who had seen the boys with Jamie yet had not intervened, and on connections between violence in the media and on the streets. The public reaction in the aftermath of murder perpetrated by children on a toddler was one of deep shock. Ravenhill wanted to 'try to write differently' from the previous generation of playwrights, to 'write within the fracture that happened to me – and I think to the society around me – in 1993' (2004: 310).

'Spin' and skewed perspectives

Playwright David Edgar proposes that 'reports of the collapse of new theatre writing' in Britain in the late 1980s/early 1990s 'had been greatly exaggerated' (Edgar, 1999: 22). One reason for this exaggeration was to prove a point against the perceived brutalism against the arts by Thatcherism – it was not expedient for theatre to promote its vitality. Thus, it can be argued that the narrative created around UK theatre in the 1980s and 1990s had its roots in the politics of theatre as an organization. Vera Gottlieb, for example, observes that theatre itself became politicized in response to threat, as distinct from staging political plays (Gottlieb and Chambers, 1999: 206). The Conservative governments from 1979 to 1997 *had* made severe cuts to theatre funding, though theatre probably was 'only experiencing the same financial pressures as other areas of the public sector – particularly health, education and local government – and was treated to the same introductions of business practices intended to ensure greater fiscal responsibility', but this shift 'inevitably affected both the subsidized theatre's sense of status and the nature of its product' (Peacock, 1999: 60–1). The Labour government under Blair is widely regarded as equally concerned with product and profit as the two preceding Conservative governments (see Peacock, 1999; Rabey, 2003). Certainly, there was an impetus for high-impact theatre during these years, as is clear in the currency of terminology: 'bums on seats', 'block-buster musicals' and 'event theatre'.

Indeed, *Blasted* has been described as being caught up in the 'event culture' (Chambers, 2002: 249), for 'when theatres grew more businesslike, hype became part of their repertoire' (Sierz, 2001a: 236). In essence, the BritPack is seen to combine 'bolshy and plaintive' (Jenkins, 2007) reactions to growing up through the 1970s–1980s with the positive vibe (political 'spin') that was given to arts and culture in the wake of transition to a Labour government during the mid-1990s. As the 1990s drew to a close, this meant it *seemed* that new playwriting talent was suddenly so prolific that it became hard to see the wood for the trees. By the time Dominic Dromgoole compiled *The Full Room: An A–Z of Contemporary Playwriting* (2000) there were more than enough writers for an alphabet.

2 Analysis and commentary

This chapter is a study of *Blasted* both as a dramatic text and as a performed play that has excited analysis and comment. A plot summary is included to present the action of the play, before undertaking a broader analysis of its characters, influences, images, themes and key scenes.

Plot summary

Ian has invited Cate to an expensive hotel in Leeds. Upon entering, Ian avails himself of the *en suite* facilities and the mini-bar, and is scathing about the quality of the room, saying that he has 'shat in better places than this' (1: 3). While he is out of sight, taking a bath, Cate relishes the opportunity to explore the room, enjoying the flowers and bounciness of the bed.

Ian is a forty-five-year-old tabloid journalist and Cate, at twenty-one, is barely half his age. From the dialogue, it becomes evident that some time ago they were involved in a relationship, which Ian is attempting to rekindle given that Cate has agreed to meet him for a night at the hotel. He is persistent in his attempts to shift events into sexual territory, using various strategies of manipulation. He plays on Cate's insecurities, telling her that she is stupid and, to the opposite extreme, saying that he loves her – even, at one point, mentioning marriage (1: 6). She says that she does not love him because he has changed, and that she does not want to have sex with him because she is not his girlfriend anymore (1: 15). She has a new boyfriend now, who is called Shaun, though she has yet to sleep with him (1: 16). Cate lives at home with her parents. She mentions her recently returned – and, by implication through the recurrence of her fits, abusive – father (1: 10), and her brother who has learning difficulties (1: 5). Ian is divorced, his wife Stella having 'fucked off with a dyke' (1: 19). He has a son, Matthew, who is twenty-four.

On two occasions, Ian upsets Cate to the extent that she has a seizure, which manifests as hysterical laughter followed by a collapse into unconsciousness. The first time this happens, Ian is helpless and has no idea what to do (1: 9). He is particularly disturbed by the likeness of Cate's fit to dying, which his own ill health makes him fear. The damage done by his persistent smoking and drinking is clear from his terrible cough, and he is caused to bend double at the pain in his 'heart, liver and kidneys' (2: 24). The second time Cate has a fit the event is more familiar to him through repetition and, recognizing the opportunity to take advantage of her temporarily altered state, '*he puts the gun to her head, lies between her legs, and simulates sex*' (2: 27).

Although Cate claims that she agreed to come to the hotel only because Ian sounded unhappy and she was worried (1: 4), certain episodes present the complexities of her feelings and show her responding to Ian as a lover. The most vivid example is in scene two '*very early the following morning*' (2: 24). It is complicated by the fact that the indications are that Ian has raped Cate during the night. He says she 'make[s] him feel safe' and he gives her reasons why he broke off their relationship, implying that her life was in danger as his 'phone was being tapped' (2: 28–9). In response to these admissions, Cate massages Ian and kisses his back, then fellates him – though, moments later she '*bites his penis as hard as she can*' (2: 31) because, as he ejaculates, he announces he is a killer (2: 30). The authenticity of his claim is never clear. Ian gets a kick out of touting the gun he carries in an underarm holster, and, as discussed further in the Character Analysis section, it is not easy to ascertain the level of truth behind his heroic posturing. Certainly, in scene three, the Soldier exposes Ian's claimed experience as incomparable with the real horrors of war.

So it is that the gun is a bridge with the second plotline, presaging Ian's fears, which are realized with the arrival of the Soldier, not very long after Cate has noted that outside the window it 'looks like there's a war on' (2: 33). From the start, the shifting and often tense atmosphere between Ian and Cate has been in counterpoint to – or perhaps even interrupted by – Ian's anticipation of external hostilities. A knocking at the door (1: 6), the phone ringing (1: 12) and, in one instance, a car backfiring in the street outside (2: 28) startles him. On the first three occasions, door knocking signals the arrival of room service: a tray of sandwiches (1: 6), a bottle of gin (1: 17) and then, the next morning, two English breakfasts (2: 35).

In the morning, while Cate is off in the bathroom, there is another knocking at the door. This time, Ian knocks back and receives replies in kind (2: 35–6). This pattern seems to satisfy him and he opens the door. The Soldier comes in, carrying a sniper's rifle. He takes Ian's gun, eats the bacon in Ian's hand and then pulls out the breakfasts from under the bed. He tells Ian that he can smell sex in the room and, finding Cate's knickers, rubs them over his face, smelling them. He goes into the bathroom and discovers that Cate has left through the window. Then he urinates on the pillow, literally marking the territory he has claimed verbally with the phrase 'our town now' (2: 39). There is a blinding light and a huge explosion as the hotel is hit by a bomb. Scene three begins with a hole in the wall with dust still falling. Ian calls out for his mother. The Soldier regains consciousness and checks whether he is still in one piece. He drinks the last few remaining drops of the gin, making Ian chuckle 'worse than me' (3: 40), and smokes a cigarette. The dialogue and events that follow present the Soldier as having committed far worse atrocities than Ian, but, contextually, demand a terrible justification for his behaviour as he perpetrates violence that is a repetition of that dealt to his girlfriend Col, who was murdered by a soldier. The Soldier rapes Ian and then sucks out and eats his eyes, describing how a solider did this to Col. His words 'poor bastard. Poor love. Poor fucking bastard' seem to embrace both Col and her assailant (3: 50). The Soldier is transferring Col onto Ian, not only in an act of retribution by replicating the atrocities to which she was subjected, but also as an act of love, kissing Ian very tenderly on the lips, his eyes closed; earlier the Soldier explained that he closes his eyes to see Col (3: 42). He is *'crying his heart out'* (3: 49), recognizing those elements of Ian that remind him of Col, particularly the smell of her cigarettes. But mostly, there is the desire to tell his story, and it is for such a purpose that he needs people like Ian: 'that's your job [as a journalist] . . . proving it happened' (3: 47). The Soldier describes the violated bodies of victims of war crimes, adding to Ian, 'can't get tragic about your arse' (3: 50).

When the lights come up on scene four, the Soldier has blown his brains out. Cate enters via the bathroom, soaking wet and carrying a baby. Seeing Ian, she reiterates in a different context the phrase 'you're a nightmare' (4: 51), which she used earlier to counteract Ian's accusations that she has led him on (2: 33). Trying to get Cate to stay, Ian repeats his underhand tactics by saying that Shaun will no longer want her as his girlfriend because he will smell the sex on her and so will perceive her to be 'soiled goods' (4: 52). Without Ian being able to see, she takes the bullets out of the gun when he asks to be given it. She tells him that that it is 'wrong to kill yourself', that 'God wouldn't like it' (4: 54 and 55). Ian says that there is no God, to which Cate replies that there has 'got to be something' because it 'doesn't make sense otherwise', to which Ian retorts that it 'doesn't make sense anyway' (4: 55). He puts the gun in his mouth and pulls the trigger. But of course it is empty, to which he responds, 'Fuck' (4: 56). When Cate says that this is 'fate' and begins to mention 'God – ' Ian interrupts with 'the cunt' (4: 57). Then, Cate notices that the baby is dead – at which Ian observes 'lucky bastard' (4: 57). Cate has a hysterical laughing fit.

As scene five begins, Cate is burying the baby under the floorboards. Then she makes to leave, and does not answer when Ian asks how she plans to get food off a soldier. She says 'why not?' when he says 'don't do that' (5: 58). He says 'that's not you' to which she replies 'I'm hungry', and he calls after her 'if you get some food – fuck' (5: 59), because the request implicates him in condoning the act of prostitution that he has just asked her not to undertake. While she is away, Ian is alone and tormented. Passing time marked by desperate actions punctuated by darkness: masturbation, self-strangulation, defecation, hysterical laughter, crying, hugging the soldier's body, lying still, eating the baby and culminates in Ian occupying the baby's grave, until at last he *dies with relief* (5: 60). Rain is coming through the roof, falling on his head. Cate enters, blood seeping between her legs, but carrying bread, sausage and gin. Her reaction to Ian could be interpreted as fondness or ridicule: 'you're sitting under a hole', 'get wet', 'stupid bastard' (5: 60). She eats and then she feeds him. It is the resurrected Ian who, with his 'thank you' in the closing moment, is at last able to show gratitude (5: 61).

Character analysis

After incessant demands that his bodily appetites be satisfied, Ian emerges in the final line of the play to appreciate the basic rations that Cate shares with him. Cate returns to the hotel from the war-torn streets not only having survived but also bringing food. Earlier, telling Ian 'mum gives me money' when he accuses her of 'still screwing the taxpayer' (1: 8), Cate appears to possess very little sense of her prospects (1: 21). It is tempting to extend this economic naivety into a more generalized innocence – which is one of the traps the characterization sets for complacent spectators, especially as Cate grows in strength during the play; a very weak positioning at the outset emphasizes this journey.

Certainly, from their first entrance, it is easy to situate Ian and Cate as absolute opposites. Kane gives the two characters a number of binary characteristics: particularly her pleasure in contrast to his cynicism. Ian claims to have 'shat in better places than this' (1: 3) yet Cate is '*amazed at the classiness of the room*' (1: 3). Equally, though Cate is transported by masturbation, she does not feel the need to drink or smoke. In contrast, Ian finds it hard to achieve even brief satisfaction through sex, alcohol and cigarettes, to the extent that every escape, even death, provides only temporary relief. His are the kind of life-threatening habits adopted by what Al Alvarez calls chronic suicides:

> These are the people who will do everything to destroy themselves, except admit that is what they are after; they will, that is, do everything except take the final responsibility for their actions . . . the alcoholics and drug addicts who kill themselves slowly and piecemeal, all the while protesting that they are merely taking the necessary steps to make an intolerable life tolerable. (1971: 155)

Ian's cigarettes and gin are literally his 'props' (Iball, 2005: 325–6 for further discussion). He is as committed a meat eater as Cate is a vegetarian, as evidenced both through the fuss over the room service sandwiches previously (1: 7) and, later, the smell of the meat-heavy English breakfasts that causes her to retch (2: 35). These binaries appear to correspond with gender stereotypes. Ian is the carnivorous red-blooded male whose 'cock aches' to ejaculate (1: 15). Indeed, *Blasted* sets up its victim/good girl, Cate, and perpetrator/bad man, Ian, and uses these archetypes in a manner adjacent to the way Kane uses box-set realism: that is, to explode our assumptions and facilitate a more complex scenario. Indeed, the critic Aleks Sierz proposes that the destabilization of comfortable binaries is a characteristic of 'in-yer-face' theatre (2001a: 6. Also see: Aston, 2003; Urban, 2001). The production history of _Blasted_ provides evidence to suggest that audience and, indeed, practitioner perception is not always sufficiently acute to recognize this strategy. One key example is the tendency to interpret Cate simply as a 'victim' – as the director Ostermeier labels his interpretation of her (2006c) – in an echo of the 'apple blossom-cheeked waif' described by one critic (Kingston, 1995). Similarly, Ian makes assumptions about Cate based on her brother's recognized special needs: pitying her mum for having 'two of you like it' (1: 5).

The bigotry inherent in Ian's attitudes is also manifest in his racism, which he demonstrates in his remarks about the hotel staff. He says that he hates Leeds because it 'stinks. Wogs and Pakis taking over' (1: 4). To bolster his own ascendancy, Ian positions himself against stereotypes, using derogatory labels for all those around him. Described at the beginning of the play as '_Welsh born but lived in Leeds all his life and picked up the accent_' (1: 3), Ian does not recognize the irony of his 'immigration' to Yorkshire, or that he wavers between identifying as Welsh or English depending on which is most expedient within the current circumstance. Cate is more than equipped to notice the ludicrous limits of Ian's perspective. So, for example, given that he believes football is tribalism, Cate queries the logical extension of this attitude: 'I go to Elland Road sometimes. Would you bomb me?' (1: 20). It is the third character in _Blasted_, the Soldier, who forces Ian to confront his myopia – in a manner that culminates in the classic convention, seen in Sophocles' _Oedipus Rex_ and Shakespeare's _King Lear_, of a literal blinding that enables insight. Indeed, _Blasted_ is structured through two key pairings of characters: Cate and Ian, Ian and the Soldier. A later section of this chapter undertakes a close analysis of key scenes, and makes detailed reference to the interweaving of these pairings.

In his introduction to *Sarah Kane: Complete Plays,* David Greig describes the tripartite identity 'Victim. Perpetrator. Bystander' (231), expressed in *4.48 Psychosis* as a 'division which catalyses the play' and suggests that 'one can see that this division is itself a culmination of ideas in the four previous plays'. *Blasted*'s Ian, for example 'is a journalist bystander who becomes a perpetrator and, finally, a victim' and he suggests that 'in Kane's writing the three figures, always contained within the single body, serve as an honest and compassionate anatomy of the human experience of pain' (xvii). While the progressive sense of this ascription is open to debate, the roles identified are resonant, and affirmed by this review of performances in the 2001 Royal Court production:

> Neil Dudgeon's Ian blends bludgeoning coarseness with a pathetic need for affection. Kelly Reilly's Cate moves astonishingly from wounded innocence to tremulous experience, while Tom Jordan Murphy's soldier is not just a bestial gun-wielder but a man driven to desperate excess. (Billington, 2001)

Also resonant is Greig's observation that Ian in *Blasted*, Hippolytus in *Phaedra's Love* and Tinker in *Cleansed*, all possess 'the same humanity that [Kane] finds in the characters who suffer [their] torments', which is a quality that renders the work 'surprisingly redemptive' (Kane, 2001: xii). Comparably, Edward Bond encapsulated the actions of the infamous baby stoners in his play *Saved* as 'the persecution of victims by victims' (1977: 15).

A pertinent extension of Greig's application of the bystander-victim-perpetrator template is to acknowledge that Cate is also a perpetrator, specifically when she bites Ian's penis '*as hard as she can*' (2: 31), but also perhaps when she flies at him slapping and hitting (2: 26), when she tears the arms from his jacket (2: 26) and when she laughs at him as he stands naked in front of her (1: 7). The critic Graham Saunders goes as far as to say that she is 'far from being an epitome of simple goodness' though this observation is qualified as 'she exacts revenge on Ian several times in retaliation against his abuse'. Saunders references the attacks listed and also notes that she ignores Ian when he is in pain and refuses to pray for him (2002: 68–9). Yet such is the variegation of their relationship that it incorporates provocative qualities in Cate's personality, as well as the reactive ones identified by Saunders. Recognizing this complexity allows that a female character can be multi-dimensional rather than archetypal, overriding the tendency to read Cate through the 'soft and clean' iconicity that Ian reads for Col (3: 48). It is here that Kane's screenplay *Skin* provides a useful point of reference as it shows graphically Marcia's physical abuse of Billy. It is also worth noting that Cate is 'not . . . [Ian's] girlfriend anymore' (1: 15) not because she walked away from exploitation but because he dropped contact with her. There are, however, aspects of the physical relationship that she does not like: she responds to kissing but demands that Ian desist from putting his tongue in her mouth (1: 12), and she does not want to proceed to intercourse (1: 14).

The relationship between Ian and Cate in the first two scenes is characterized by something of a mating ritual of advance and retreat, one in which possession of the upper hand varies. The audience is encouraged to make assumptions and then those assumptions are challenged, facilitating a more subtle understanding of sexual engagement between female adolescents and (middle-aged) adult males. While Cate is twenty-one, the play implies that the relationship has been going on since she was an adolescent. In sociological study of such relationships, research has identified a discourse of romance in which the women are looking for a 'romantic hero' who 'displays a strong sexual desire held in check by tenderness and an understanding of the heroine's emotional needs (Leahy, 1994: 56). One young woman describes how part of the transition into sexual activity was to look for a partner with experience, who sought to arouse but also was prepared to stop when an encounter became too passionate. She felt that the treatment she received from older lovers was far better than she would get from boys of her own age (56). However, participation in such relationships is socially constructed as 'harmful to the younger parties involved' (50) particularly as 'voluntary intergenerational sex is seen as precocious sexualization' (52). This is because 'emphasised femininity' is 'an ideal of conduct' promoted in a mass media 'organised, financed and supervised by men' (Leahy, 1994: 49). In *Blasted*, Ian is seen to participate in this ideal on several occasions which highlight the double-standards fuelling it – he believes he has license to engage Cate in sexual activity, yet he is 'embarrassed' when Cate mentions that she touches herself (1: 22–3), and he does not want her to sell her body to soldiers in exchange for food: 'that's not you' (5: 59).

In *Blasted*, the difficulty in establishing clear, or consistent, distinctions between sexual and platonic relations is brought to the fore. Love and violence, not simply sex and violence, are co-habitants in complex rather than wholly abusive inter-character relations. This is expressed vividly in the Soldier's combined tenderness and torture as he rapes Ian, at the same time reliving making love with Col. The coupling of love and violence is also inherent in Cate and Ian's relationship, contentious because it is sometimes tender, sometimes fraught, often ambivalent – not least because of its retrospective implication of paedophilia.

Influences, genre and style

It was Bill Buford's book on football hooliganism – *Among the Thugs* – that led Kane to *King Lear* partway into her writing process, as she worked on Ian's delirium through the construction of vivid theatrical images (Saunders, 2002: 61). Describing an incident of football violence that Kane drew upon directly, Buford proposed that the eye sucking exceeded 'even Shakespeare in his own excesses; after all, Gloucester had his eyes pulled out by hand' (1991: 242).

This example illustrates how necessary it is to keep dramatic influences upon Kane in perspective. *Blasted* self-consciously invokes the distinctive styles of a sequence of landmark dramatists – Pinter and Ibsen, Brecht, and Beckett (Sierz, 2001a: 102) – yet, as James Macdonald observes, while 'her theatrical gods were Beckett, Pinter, Bond, Potter' she 'wrote directly from her own experience and from her heart'. This is a quality of engagement that he identifies in the direct connections between her playwriting and her love of music, observing that she borrows lines from 'Joy Division, the Pixies, Ben Harper, Radiohead, Polly Harvey, the Tindersticks, even Elvis Presley' (Macdonald, 1999).

The neo-punk band Joy Division is reputed to have formed after attending a 1976 Sex Pistols gig in Manchester. The contradictions and compulsions of relationships are encapsulated in the title of one of Joy Division's best-known songs: *Love Will Tear Us Apart [Again]* (1979). The band took their name from the corps of young women kept in a Nazi concentration camp for the pleasure of officers on leave, which they had read about in Karol Cetinsky's book *The House of Dolls* (1956). An extract from the book is recited in their song *No Love Lost*. *Blasted* foregrounds the habitual sexual abuse of women, within and without war.

Kane craved a theatre whose audience engaged as actively as one would at a football match, pop concert or a live sex show such as one she described seeing in Amsterdam (1998b). Her quest was inspired by a theatre event that she witnessed as life changing and 'totally experiential' (Sierz, 2001a: 92). Jeremy Weller's *Mad* (Grassmarket, 1992), which she saw on the Edinburgh Festival Fringe, was a piece of devised and confessional theatre in which a group of performers, predominantly female, talked about their personal relationships, their experiences of clinical depression and the treatment they had received. The raw honesty of *Mad* – very much echoed in Kane's *Sick* monologues – is present in the complex machinations and shifting vulnerabilities of Ian and Cate's relationship in the opening scenes of *Blasted*. Kane showed an early draft of this material to her friend Vincent O'Connell, upon whose recommendation she re-read Edward Bond's *Saved* (see Sierz, 2001a: 101). Although it was to the infamous baby-stoning scene in *Saved* that a number of critics and commentators referred when confronted with the violent acts in *Blasted*, it should also be noted that Bond's play, like *Blasted*, begins with the sparring mating ritual of a couple – and it was, in fact, the spareness and tautness of Bond's dialogue that inspired Kane when she began to edit. Like *King Lear*, *Saved* became influential to Kane partway through writing *Blasted*. She was later to describe Bond as her 'major inspiration' (Saunders, 2002: 24).

Equally, the opening scenes of *Blasted* invoke Harold Pinter's drama, showing the threat outside the room throwing into relief the individuals in conflict within it. They use stage properties and the characters' engagement with their environment, employing the apparently 'casual' realism of the stage properties to create symbolic 'stations' within the plot (States, 1985: 67), in a manner akin to the naturalist strategies of Ibsen. These scenes also echo some of Ibsen's recurrent themes of disease in the body (*Ghosts*, 1881) and in society, and the infantilization of women by a patriarchal society (*A Dolls House*, 1879; *Hedda Gabler*, 1890). In common with Pinter, Cate and Ian's verbal sparring is minimal and rhythmic, with silences written into the script. Their half-explained relationship has an underlying sinister sexual charge; the air heavy with threat. This is often manifested in the liminal areas of the space – those that give access to the room. It is a strategy reminiscent of Pinter's *The Dumbwaiter* (1958), particularly through the tense humour of the door knocking sequence (*Blasted*, 2: 35–6).

Alongside the named dramatists, playwrights such as Caryl Churchill, Phyllis Nagy and Martin Crimp, in constantly reinventing form and looking to European traditions for ideas, provide theatrical guidance for Kane and those playwrights who have been aligned with her – rather than the epic pedagogic dramas of the 1970s and 1980s by writers such as David Hare and David Edgar (see Urban, 2001). To the list of dramatists mentioned so far should be added Howard Barker, whose *Arguments for a Theatre* (1993 [1989]) provided a very inspiring manifesto for drama students in the 1990s and who, along with Howard Brenton and Peter Barnes, was, tagged a 'New Jacobean' (Taylor, 1971: 24). Indeed, as an undergraduate student Kane had played the main role of 'Bradshaw' in Howard Barker's *Victory* (1983). In this play, Barker's habitual fascination with human behaviour in crisis situations, and particularly in their aftermath, is expressed in Bradshaw's journey to gather the scattered remains of her husband who has been executed by supporters of Charles II. Here is a determination in the face of brutal opposition that is concordant with Cate's fortitude in *Blasted*.

Phyllis Nagy's conception of the writer carrying around her influences like a pocketful of change (Saunders, 2002: 154) is an effective simile, and good defence against the temptation to privilege literary influences over a wider range of creative inspiration. For example, Buford asserts that 'there is no sport in which the act of being a spectator is as *constantly* physical as watching a game of English football on the terraces' adding that 'you could feel the anticipation of the crowd on all sides of your body as a series of sensations' (Buford, 1991: 166, 168). Kane liked to compare the experience of theatregoing with that of spectatorship at a match – as she did in a newspaper article titled 'Drama with Balls' in 1998. She played this comparison when called to defend *Blasted* in the aftermath of critical attack: 'the level of analysis that you listen to on the terraces is astonishing. If people did that in the theatre . . . but they don't. They expect to sit back and not participate' (Benedict, 1995).

It is in relation to Expressionism that Kane's 'experiential' intent is cast in a particular light. Expressionism's fundamental tenets situate 'the body as an expressive locus of suffering' and extend 'internal impulses onto external forms, especially landscapes' (Cardinal 1984: 42 and 38). Kane loved the work of Georg Büchner, directing his play *Woyzeck,* generally recognized as the first German Expressionist drama; its episodic structure is echoed in Kane's *Cleansed.* Indeed, 'Expressionism imploded realism's composition, blowing up the inner life until its outer frames snapped' (Fleche, 1997: 89) and, in something of a prefiguration of *Blasted,* August Stramm's 1915 Expressionist play *Awakening* climaxes in the destruction of its hotel room set.

The central section of *Blasted* is the catalyst for the transformation of Ian and Cate's relationship. Here, Kane employs Brechtian distancing (*Verfremdungseffect*) to challenge the 'conventional resemblance between the performer's body' and 'the character to which it refers' (Diamond, 1997: 45) – for example, the Soldier describes what happened to Col while he enacts it upon Ian. From this episode onwards, Ian progressively loses agency over his body as *Blasted* moves from the sheer force of the bomb blast not to a majestic flood like the one that extinguishes the flames in Stramm's *Awakening* but to a torturous Beckettian drip of water from the shattered hotel roof that refuses to let him rest in peace. Ian's desperate behaviour is, as with the characters in Beckett's *Play* (1963), switched on and off by the stage light. In the final sequence of *Blasted,* Ian is trapped in the manner of Beckett's tragic-comic figures, able to do nothing but sit and wait, while Cate negotiates a war zone. In a scenario reminiscent of work by Howard Barker where 'catastrophe is also birth' (1995: 180), Ian expresses a dawning gratitude in his final words of 'thank you' (5: 61) to Cate.

Close reading of key scenes

A significant factor in the impact of *Blasted* is the way that Kane has pared away at her material until it has a tautness of dramatic and theatrical structure, which enables the dialogue to seem very intensely situated in the present moment. This quality of the dialogue, in relation to theatrical images that are striking in their clarity, contributes to and is dependent on the matrix of themes and imagery resonating throughout the play. Indeed, in response to the furore against the premiere, Kane accused critics of ignoring the image structure (Saunders, 2002: 46). The play demands of its practitioners and audiences that the latticework of connections be recognized. Thus, it is useful to undertake close analysis in a way that acknowledges the intricate warp and weft Kane took pains to construct. The play demands that its audience read between the scenes and between the lines. What is evident is that the scene changes are precisely that: changes *within themselves*, in that something cataclysmic occurs in the blackout; the blackout is not a simple punctuation. The 'blasts' – penetrating Cate, devastating the room, visiting suicide upon the Soldier – occur between scenes, the staged action recommencing in the immediate aftermath, when the bodied space is reeling from the shock. So the units of text that straddle the scene changes are of particular interest in representing anticipation and aftermath, as the following sections explore.

Rips before the blast (1: 22–2: 27)

As the first scene draws to a close, the complex wrangling between Ian and Cate has been distilled to its essence. Ian's attempts at reciprocity 'Make love to me . . . [I'll] make love to you' (1: 22) are met with Cate's refusal, expressed as 'can't': she 'can't' make love to him because she does not love him anymore, and she 'can't' make him 'happy' (1: 23), just as earlier she has said she 'can't' eat meat. The scene concludes with the stark contrast between Ian's assertion 'I love you' and Cate's response 'I don't love you' (1: 24). As Kane makes clear, the 'stage directions function as lines' (2) and the scene ends with an attempt at a chivalrous gesture from Ian who, at Cate's retort, '*Turns away . . . sees the bouquet of flowers and picks them up*' – "these are for you"' (1: 24). The inappropriate timing of this action underlines how Ian's sexual directness is coupled awkwardly with a rather sentimental attempt at gentlemanly behaviour that earlier has led him to suggest marriage (1: 6). Indeed, Ian justifies and elevates aspects of his behaviour by claiming that he acts in the name of love: for his country (1: 30; 2: 32–3; 3: 41; 3: 45) and for Cate (1: 5–6; 1: 17; 1: 20; 1: 22–4; 2: 27; 2: 31; 4: 51). The conflation of love and sex is cheapened by its context as part of Ian's battery of attempts to persuade Cate to have sex. It is devalued further by Ian's reasoning: 'Don't know nothing. That's why I love you, want to make love to you' (1: 23).

Scene two begins '*very early the following morning*' and the setting is '*the same*' except that '*the bouquet of flowers is now ripped apart and scattered around the room*' (2: 24). Patterning in the play is clear here: scene one ends with the flowers, scene two begins with their wreckage – the implication of 'deflowerment' through rape is confirmed as the scene progresses by Cate's anger and disgust, and from the inference of Ian's line 'we're one, yes?' (2: 26). There is also a subtle connection from the bouquet back to the opening of the play, when Cate explores the room as soon as Ian has gone to the bathroom and she is alone. Then, the first word she speaks is 'lovely' in response to seeing the flowers, which have made her smile (1: 4). As in the opening scene, the first thing Ian does in scene two is to get a gin. On this occasion, the effect is immediate and he is 'overcome with pain' at the first sip, and then he begins to cough '*each cough tearing at his lung*' (2: 24) until '*just at the moment when it seems he cannot survive this, it begins to ease*' (2: 25). This suffering was previously hidden in the privacy of the *en suite* bathroom in scene one. Here, its visibility is emphasized by the fact that Cate '*wakes and watches Ian*' (2: 24) and, after '*very slowly, the pain decreases until it has all gone*' he '*looks up and sees Cate watching him*'. As in the first scene, Cate's silent observation is broken by a single word from her: here 'cunt' (2: 25), which is a vivid insult evocative of the reductive male sexual fantasies expressed in the later incantation of the word, which is repeated eleven times in a row as Ian masturbates (5: 59).

The flowers as a material by which Ian constructs his romantic gestures, undercut by a crass and unrestrained sexual appetite, express the devastation he visits upon Cate and which, later, in exaggerated form, is visited upon him. She rejects his 'gift' by shredding the bouquet and then performs a symbolic mutilation in much closer approximation of actual bodily harm later in the scene. Ian has thrown the gun on the bed having deflated the impact of revenge with 'don't worry, I'll be dead soon' and suggesting that Cate 'have a pop'. When she does not move, he '*chuckles and goes into the bathroom*' (2: 25). She takes his absence as an opportunity to dress and pack her bag. Kate Ashfield who played the character at the Royal Court describes how people said they were angry that Cate did not seize that opportunity to leave – but Ashfield justifies it by saying she 'stay[s] to hurt Ian' (Saunders, 2002: 164). She smells Ian's leather jacket, an action which is ambiguous in its connection to the pleasure of familiar scent, to Ian's preoccupation with the need to wash away his 'stink' and to the vacillations between engagement and discord in their relationship. She rips the arms from his leather jacket. On his return, Ian suggests they go for breakfast because 'it's paid for' (2: 26) and the resonances here are of his expectation that he will take what he perceives to be his dues out of situations, just as he expects sex from Cate because she has come to the hotel. Ian putting on the jacket and experiencing its damage is a catalyst for Cate who flies at Ian and slaps him around the head '*hard and fast*' until he 'wrestles her onto the bed' and she 'takes the gun from his holster and points it at his groin' causing him to 'back . . . off rapidly' (2: 26). She goes into a fit, and he *'puts the gun to her head, lies between her legs, and stimulates sex'* until *'as he comes, CATE sits bolt upright with a shout'* (2: 27). She laughs hysterically until she collapses. In productions of *Blasted* by Graeae (UK tour and London, 2006–7) and by Ostermeier (Berlin, 2005) the audience laughed at Ian's humping and grinding, undermining his apparently powerful exploitative position.

Kane, like Beckett, has a well-honed sense of the tragic-comic, which is also seen when Ian stands naked in front of Cate and demands fellatio – a demand that provokes laughter from Cate (and the audience) and sinks Ian into embarrassment, which sends him fumbling off the stage to dress (1: 8). Writing a review of the 2001 Royal Court production of *Blasted*, Andrew Smith observed 'you're often unsure whether they're laughing or crying on stage and Kane's singular gift as a dramatist is to make you, the audience, feel like doing both at the same time' (2001).

In scene two, the audience witness Ian stranded by such reactions, in the manifestations of Cate's fit:

As he comes, CATE sits bolt upright with a shout. IAN moves away, unsure what to do, pointing the gun at her from behind. She laughs hysterically, as before, but doesn't stop. She laughs and laughs and laughs until she isn't laughing any more, she's crying her heart out. (2: 27)

As before, Ian is unsure how to respond, at first pointing the gun at her and then kissing her until she comes round. Cate tells him she wants to go home, he tries to persuade her to stay until 'after breakfast' and when she refuses *'locks the door and pockets the key'* saying 'I love you' (2: 27). He denies her freedom, and while she arrived at the hotel of her own volition, he has shifted the dynamic.

Ian drives Cate to seek solace in the bathroom, and this provides her means of escape when he inadvertently opens the door to the Soldier.

Ian and someone worse (2: 39–3: 44 and 3: 49–4: 50)

HELEN IBALL: We were talking about how the explosion happens in that scene between you and Ian. It's a pivotal scene in the play, even the focus of it, given the title. Were you aware of that when you played it? You talked to me at Scarborough about watching Ian and Cate at the beginning and having a sense of Ian from the beginning, and then you enter into it . . . what do you think the purpose of the Soldier is – what does he reveal about Ian that Cate doesn't?

DAVID TOOLE: I think Ian constantly is like this big 'I am' until I come along and go 'but you haven't done that, you're all talk, you're not the man you think you are'. . .

HELEN IBALL: Is Ian some kind of government agent?

DAVID TOOLE: I was never convinced whether Ian convinced himself, lived in this little fantasy world and was trying to convince Cate that he was, or whether he *actually* was, I don't know. That always seemed vague to me. I don't think it's clear cut . . . and I think that's why, when the soldier comes, that's when he gets found out . . . that he's not done, can't do, these things . . . (Toole, 2006a)

The hotel is blasted by a mortar bomb between scenes two and three. Moments previously, Ian's line 'if you've come to shoot me–' has been followed by the Soldier reaching out '*to touch Ian's face*' but stopping '*short of physical contact*' (3: 38). This gesture anticipates the tender sequence leading to Ian's rape (3: 49), discussed in detail later in this section. Ian's verbal recoil from touch 'You taking the piss?' is followed immediately by the Soldier's assertion 'our town now' at which he *'stands on the bed and urinates over the pillows'* (2: 39). This is Buford's description of a scene in Turin, when supporters were there to see Manchester play Juventus in the semi-final of the Cup Winner's Cup (1984):

> I looked behind me and I saw a large vehicle had been over-turned, and that further down the street flames were issuing from a building. I hadn't seen any of this happen: I realised that there had been more than I had been able to take in. There was now the sound of sirens, many sirens, different kinds, coming from several directions. The city is ours, Sammy said, and he repeated the possessive, each time with greater intensity: it is *ours, ours, ours.* (Buford, 1991: 93)

It is at this point in *Blasted* that *'There is a blinding light, then a huge explosion. Blackout. The sound of summer rain'. Scene three opens with 'the hotel has been blasted by a mortar bomb. There is a large hole in one of the walls, and everything is covered with dust which is still falling'.* When the lights come up, the Soldier is still unconscious. Immediately he comes round, the Soldier *'turns his eyes and rifle on Ian'* such is the level of threat in this war zone. He checks whether he is in one piece, then demands 'the drink' (2: 39) from Ian. Though Ian says it is empty, the Soldier *'takes the bottle and drinks the last mouthful'*, an action that makes Ian *'chuckle'* from recognition: 'worse than me' (3: 40). This observation encapsulates the function of the Soldier within the structure of the play. Literally, in the openings of the first two scenes, it was Ian seeking out immediate solace in gin. They smoke, and the Soldier comments that he has 'never met an Englishman with a gun before, most of them don't know what a gun is' – a comment that resonates in terms of Kane's motivation and purpose in writing *Blasted* as a response to the myopia and complacency she felt typified British citizens.

The Soldier is curious about Ian's identity and, having asked earlier whether he is a journalist, asks whether he is a soldier. Ian is evasive on both, admitting to being a soldier 'of sorts' (3: 40) and then correcting the Soldier who assumes he is English 'I'm Welsh' though the Soldier identifies his accent and Ian acknowledges he lives in England, and then qualifies this 'English and Welsh is the same. British. I'm not an import' because the Soldier questions whether Ian might be a 'foreigner'. Similarly, the Soldier's labelling of Ian's 'girlfriend' leads him to correct 'she's not my girlfriend' and then to tell the Soldier to mind his own business when he asks for clarification. It is on this point that the Soldier observes, 'not been here long have you' and adds, 'learn some manners, Ian' (3: 41). This implies a shift in location with the Soldier's arrival, so that the room and its occupants have been transported into a war zone, rather than the war coming to Leeds – although this distinction is immaterial and the image structure being far more significant than the specific location.

Ian does not like the Soldier using his name. The Soldier makes him uncomfortable by looking at him for 'a very long time' and then, when Ian has admitted 'my name's Ian', announces 'I/Am/ Dying to make love/Ian'. The line breaks communicate emphatic delivery through the phrasing. The Soldier asks whether Ian has a girlfriend, and then says that he has 'Col. Fucking beautiful', and describes how he closes his eyes to 'think about her' (3: 42).

The Soldier wants to know whether the sex Ian had during the night was good, but Ian says – with a dismissive machismo – that he doesn't know because he was 'pissed. Probably not'. The Soldier begins to tell of atrocities he has committed, and Ian (the journalist) says 'don't tell me', but the Soldier persists with the story – saying that the youngest he fucked was twelve years old after which he 'made her lick me clean' while he closed his eyes and 'thought of –' which invokes Col. He describes how he and his fellow soldiers shot the twelve year old's 'father in the mouth' and hung her brothers 'from the ceiling by their testicles'. The Soldier wants to know whether Ian has done similar deeds, and he denies it. The Soldier asks, 'what about [the] girl locked . . . in the bath-room' and Ian *'doesn't answer'* (3: 43). He then, childishly, admits 'you did four in one go, I've only ever done one' (3: 44) – a way of reckoning which the Soldier proceeds to undermine, in a manner that expresses the pertinence of the connection Kane made between seed and tree (Saunders, 2002: 39) mentioned in the previous chapter. The point is not that atrocities are equivalent in all contexts, but that we should be wary of our tendency to afford them different values. Indeed, 'the logical conclusion to the way society expects men to behave is war' (Urban, 2001: 66) and, fur-thermore, to annex an observation about football hooliganism from *Among the Thugs*: 'if there was a war . . . he'd be the hero' (Buford, 1991: 118).

The Soldier then connects rape and murder, by asking whether Ian was going to kill Cate. This leads Ian to reach for his gun, which the Soldier warns him against, 'don't, I'll have to shoot you. Then I'd be lonely'. He then asks why Ian didn't kill Cate given that he does not 'seem to like her very much' (3: 44). This is a telling line, as it draws attention to Ian's misogyny, the arbitrary limits to his abuse of Cate, and his unsatisfactory moral standpoint, which he is forced to question even in its annunciation 'She's . . . a woman . . . I've never – . . . It's not – ' so that when the Soldier pushes 'What?' Ian *'doesn't answer'* – the Soldier invokes the archetype that he has raised earlier, that all soldiers are bastards and that he and Ian are both soldiers. He makes it evident that there are consequences to Ian's self-valorizing claims. Indeed, it is at this point that the Soldier reveals that when he goes home there is no 'going back' to Col because 'she's dead, see. Fucking bastard soldier, he –' to which the stage direction indicates *'He stops. Silence'* (3: 44).

The Soldier's recognition of fates worse than death invokes the rupturing of human dignity through sexual abuse: 'See. Rather be shot than fucked and shot'. It prompts capitulation, a terrified, self-preserving response to the power of the gun 'and now you agree with anything I say'. When the Soldier '*kisses IAN very tenderly on the lips*' the collision of sexual abuse with a loving action is disturbing, and, as in previous moments of encounter between the Soldier and Ian, '*they stare at each other*' (3: 49. See also 2: 36 and 2: 38). The superimposition of Col onto Ian is signalled by 'you smell like her. Same cigarettes'. This is further emphasized by the stage direction that as he rapes Ian, the Soldier has his '*eyes closed . . . smelling Ian's hair*' and '*crying his heart out*'. While Ian's '*face registers pain*' he remains silent. After the rape, he '*pushes the revolver up IAN's anus*' and tells him 'bastards pulled the trigger on Col. What's it like?' The Soldier is desperate to communicate horrific experiences to the journalist. The stage directions indicate that Ian '*tries to answer. He can't*' (3: 49). A number of commentators have raised the theme of the inexpressibility of pain, and attempts to communicate it. This is discussed further in the final section of the chapter.

Reiterating Cate's early questions to Ian as to whether he has been attracted to men (1: 19), the Soldier asks Ian whether he has ever been 'fucked by a man before?' (3: 49). He takes Ian's failure to reply as an indication that he has not, and tells him 'it's nothing' and describes atrocities that he has seen, including a 'starving man eating his dead wife's leg' that anticipates the later cannibalistic behaviour by Ian. His advice is 'can't get tragic about your arse. Don't think your Welsh arse is any different to any other arse I fucked' (3: 50). This dismissive attitude is underlined by his immediate questioning as to whether Ian has any more food – and echoes Ian's focus upon breakfast in the aftermath of Cate's rape (2: 35). Then the Soldier sucks out and eats Ian's eyes, again describing this in terms of what was done to Col: 'He ate her eyes./Poor bastard./Poor love./Poor fucking bastard' (3: 50). As David Toole summarized in describing rehearsals for the role, the Soldier

> wants to find a journalist. He wants to find someone to tell the story. Then somebody said 'yeah, but do you think he hates journalists because he knows that they don't do that?' And it was like ping – light goes on. And that made it even more interesting to play. He's got to tell this story and that's why it builds up to that rape because Ian is just not getting it and the Soldier will do anything to get the story across to him. (2006a)

The previous scene closed with the Soldier's annexation of the room by urinating on the bed; here he marks his territory and his experiences on Ian's body. The critic Sean Carney comments 'as in all tragic reversals, Ian's peripeteia is full of dramatic irony: it seems that since Ian will not open his tabloid journalist's eyes to the atrocities of war, he loses his eyes altogether' (2005: 287). There is a '*blackout*' and '*the sound of autumn rain*'. Scene four begins in 'the same' setting. Between scenes the Soldier has '*blown his own brain out*' (4: 50). Cate enters through the bathroom door '*soaking wet and carrying a baby*'. She '*steps over the SOLDIER with a glance*', which might indicate that she has seen much the same on the streets outside, and his presence is thus unremarkable (4: 51).

Cate and the Soldier are never engaged with Ian at the same time and yet can seem to be in cahoots as they unravel his arrogance. Cate has ripped the sleeves from Ian's jacket, the Soldier proceeds to strip it of Ian's liberty – taking his keys, wallet and passport (2: 38). This is one stage away from his utter disassembly in scene five.

No nothing (4: 54–5: 61)
Towards the end of scene four, Ian's sensory deprivation makes him dependent on Cate. As helpless, indeed, as the baby she carries in

her arms. Ian requests assistance from her in finding his gun. Cate searches and '*sees the revolver in the SOLDIER's hand and stares at it for some time*' (4: 54). When Ian asks whether she has found it, Cate says no. The bluff and double dare around the gun – which has been present earlier in the text (1: 3; 1: 6; 1: 8; 2: 25–7; 2: 35–6) – is intensified here by Ian's vulnerability and by the fact that his behaviour displays the earnestness of desperation. He *really* wants to die now. The situation is also heightened by collusion, invoked through dramatic irony. The audience and Cate know that she has removed the bullets, while Ian's blindness excludes him from this knowledge. Thus, when Ian instructs Cate not to stand behind him, then shoots the gun repeatedly and fails, there is likely to be laughter from the audience – reminiscent of responses to Chekhovian tragi-comic moments, particularly *Uncle Vanya* (1900) whose suicide is also thwarted by pistol failure.

Ian would rather shoot himself than starve to death (4: 54) – a notional 'lesser of two evils' reminiscent of the Soldier's wry observation: 'rather be shot than fucked and shot' (3: 49). Cate states that it is wrong to shoot yourself because 'God wouldn't like it' (4: 54–5). This is part of the way she makes sense of existence, and Ian is quick to puncture it: 'no God. No Father Christmas. No fairies. No Narnia. No fucking nothing'. His nihilism equates religion with fantastical narratives from childhood. The lines are bleak and funny because of their conflation of 'serious' and 'whimsical' belief systems and also because of their witty momentum. Its double negative – 'no nothing' – also evokes a tinge of fragile hope, which is iterated in the play's closing moments. Here, as at the end, Cate's determination is admirable – she retorts that Ian 'can't give up' because that would be 'weak' (4: 55). However, though she has thwarted Ian's attempt to die, the baby slips into death in her arms without Cate noticing until it is too late. The scene ends with her hysterical laughter.

The final scene begins with Cate making a cross for the baby's grave, using the arms she tore from Ian's jacket to bind it together, and scattering the remnants of the bouquet as part of the burial ritual (5: 57). While praying for a better experience for the innocents represented by the dead baby girl (5: 58), Cate adapts to the situation in which she finds herself and leaves the room – prepared to barter her body to procure food from the soldiers on the streets outside (5: 58–9). That Ian's certainty 'when you die it's the end' (4: 56) is bravado is underlined by his request that Cate pray for him (5: 58) – and this whole sequence anticipates and adds to the significance of Ian's experiences in scene five, where the punctuation of vignettes with '*darkness. Light*' (5: 59–60) expresses not only condensed and passing time, but also the repeated interruption and thwarting of relief and ultimately oblivion. The use of blackouts is prolific and orchestrates Ian's suffering. Punctuating his frenetic actions, the blackouts heighten the tension because they seem to concentrate a much longer period of time into 'theatre-time'.

The sequence begins with Ian masturbating, his eleven repetitions of 'cunt' reducing women to the most basic denominator. Though sexual relief is achievable through auto-erotic stimulation, attempts at suicide by self-strangulation with his hands are futile. The third vignette is of Ian 'shitting and then trying to clean it up with newspaper'. The sequence expresses the abject body – its bodily functions, its spillage, its appetites. There is a grotesque connection between hysterical laughter and the nightmare that succeeds it (5: 59). The final vignette is of Ian eating the baby before reburying it under the floorboards, and then climbing in with it, his '*head poking out of the floor*' (5: 60). Carney identifies this as 'the most commonly circulated image from the play' and 'the most interpretatively rich moment in the drama'. He asserts that the image of Ian is of a man 'who is *neither* alive nor dead, or who is *both* alive and dead' and that this is 'possible only within theatre itself'. Thus 'Ian is a figure that is at once phenomenally real and entirely constituted by the imagination of the audience, who *can* see him as both alive and dead' (Carney, 2005: 293).

Changing views of the play, themes and theory

A decade on from the premiere of *Blasted*, critical analysis has reached a remarkable accord in its reading of the play's form and function. It does not seem too bold to argue that scholarship has caught up with the particular intelligence of the play itself, given that a comparative study of academic articles reveals a cumulative understanding, as this section considers. Furthermore, and with immense irony given that the play expresses an objection to British myopia and solipsism, the 7 July suicide bombings on London transport in 2005 have rendered the scenario of the play prophetic. There is a parallel to be drawn here with Caryl Churchill's *Far Away* (2000). The critic Aleks Sierz notes that the playwright 'Mark Ravenhill can justifiably argue that one of the most theatrical and thrilling responses to 9/11 was Churchill's *Far Away*, and that was first staged in November 2000, almost a year before the event' (2005: 60). A similar perception is implied in some press reviews of the Graeae tour of *Blasted* in 2006–7 through the phrase 'shock and awe'; the name given by the military to the first assault on Iraq, which subsequently has become a familiar phrase in media reports of the heightened state of terror (Fisher, 2006; Cooper, 2006). The currency of the phrase seems intended to justify the graphic content of *Blasted* by identifying a specific parallel. This attitude may be a counter-reaction to the responses *Blasted* attracted at first, with a tendency for commentators to valorize the attributes that the press had originally vilified.

The critic Sean Carney notes this initial reliance upon shock effect, from the first night press and the titles of the first major publications to address Kane: Aleks Sierz's *In-Yer-Face Theatre: British Drama Today* (2001a) and Graham Saunders' *'Love Me or Kill Me': Sarah Kane and the Theatre of Extremes* (2002). In this first phase of commentary, terminology became a litmus test that at times threatened to undermine the effectiveness of those who championed Kane's theatre. The claim upon Aleks Sierz's term 'experiential' (2001a: 4) drama – made initially by the playwright herself – was a tightrope or at worst even a trip-wire for its proponents. One of the main areas under review quickly became the extent to which the work achieves its intended experiential aesthetic.

Saunders is self-critical and re-evaluative of his monograph in the subsequent journal article '"Just a Word on a Page and there is the Drama": Sarah Kane's Theatrical Legacy' (2003). He re-chisels the revolutionary experiential model to one that is more to do with literary verve and frame, though he gets tangled with the issue of 'strict formal control' and thinks her work is 'only ever partly experiential' (2003: 100). His analysis is concerned with the insistent classification by which the play was besieged, and perhaps equally by the wish to ensure Kane received due recognition for the literary merit of her work in the face of patronizing attitudes from some members of the press. *Blasted* was described as 'the most controversial first play for years and one of immense promise' (Coveney, 1995), though elsewhere it was noted 'Kane has a lot to learn (she is 23), but I look forward to her next play to see what she has learned' (Peter, 1995). Annabelle Singer recalls a talk given to students at Royal Holloway, University of London in 1998, at which she says Kane described how, at the premiere, 'all but five of the audience members were critics, and all but three of the critics were white middle-aged men' (2004: 145). Even now, some reviewers continue to display a tendency to cheapen the text and what they perceive as its core audience, from whom they separate themselves with statements such as:

> The play still doesn't strike me as a masterpiece – it's too glib and derivative for that – but it will always have a strong appeal for anguished adolescents trying to make sense of the world, and

it does at least end on a note of compassion. Goths and emos should book now. (Spencer, 2006)

Such a suggestion of immaturity is at odds with the view shared by a number of commentators that *Blasted* makes a powerful and distinctive response to contemporary politics and society.

Tragic paradoxes

The playwright Howard Brenton believes that *Blasted* is the only recent stage play to encapsulate ideas propounded by the eminent cultural theorist Terry Eagleton in *Sweet Violence: The Idea of the Tragic* (2002). In this book, Eagleton proposed a new theory of tragedy for our contemporary age. His ideas are, in part, a response to the widely accepted assertion, represented by George Steiner's *The Death of Tragedy* (1961), that tragic form is redundant in a secular and rational society where notions of fate, vengeance and repentance have ceased to be meaningful. Eagleton's idea of the contemporary tragic is situated in the close proximity between our society's insistence upon the freedom of the individual and the deep anguish of profound loneliness. This connection is driven by what Eagleton describes as the self-mutilation at the root of civilization. The link between Ian in *Blasted* and this conception of the tragic is clear, particularly as the facilities of this expensive hotel room (the mini-bar especially) contribute to his suffering – as does his egocentricity, which makes him dismissive of other perspectives until they are, quite literally, forced upon him by the Soldier. Furthermore, Brenton draws a parallel between Kane's play and the qualities of Eagleton's new tragic form in terms of 'the strange sweetness of an aesthetic spectacle with suffering at its core' (2002). There is consensus among a significant number of commentators that this quality, which they describe in a variety of ways, is the essence of *Blasted*. Their assertions tend to focus on the final scene of the play, and particularly its closing moments when Cate returns to the devastated hotel room – bleeding but bringing food and drink – to find Ian blinded and almost buried, the drips of water from the leaking roof merging with the blood on his face.

Aleks Sierz identifies the reversal that occurs in *Blasted* as Ian becomes dependent and Cate grows into a survivor. As Sierz notes, it is through this reversal that the play asserts the possibility of something beautiful emerging out of despair (2001a: 91). This scenario is very much in accord with the application of an 'ethics of catastrophe' to *Blasted*. The critic Ken Urban observes that, like the playwright Howard Barker who asserts that 'catastrophe is also birth' (1995: 180), Kane creates a theatre that does not offer solutions or redemption but rather 'the possibility that an ethics can exist between wounded bodies, that after devastation, good becomes possible' (Urban, 2001: 37). Similarly, Graham Saunders draws upon Jonathan Dollimore's conception of the 'tragic paradox' – of dignity arising from debasement – to observe that at the moment when Ian might be 'expected to be most brutalised he becomes most human' (2004: 73) in his grateful response to Cate's decision to return to the room and feed him.

Ethical spaces

Ken Urban encapsulates the import of the play's closing images when he observes that Ian's final line 'thank you' is 'not a moment of moral redemption, but, instead, a call for an ethical means of being in the world' (2001: 66). This distinction is important, and connects directly with Eagleton's proposals regarding new tragic form, as summarized in the section above. It situates *Blasted* as an incisive and effective response to contemporary international relations. The notion of moral redemption invokes repentance and forgiveness for misdemeanours in the context of an authorized code of right and wrong – for example, religious doctrine relating to sin and absolution within Christian faiths. Moral viewpoints based on such belief systems are socially and culturally specific, which cause them to exclude and judge others, whereas an 'ethical means of being in the world' is about fostering a respect for the dignity of each person that acknowledges global diversity in cultures and beliefs.

Blasted has been described as a 'severe indictment of ethical apathy' (Wixson, 2005: 85), making its case through the disruption of dramatic conventions and the unsettling effect this disruption has upon an audience, especially as it is coupled with sexual and violent acts. The Soldier insists 'imagine it' when Ian says he 'can't imagine' the level of atrocity that is being described, andhe pushes Ian to 'imagine harder' (3: 45). In a manner that can be seen to parallel this scenario, a number of commentators (e.g. Iball, 2005; Sakellaridou, 1999; Wixson, 2005) pay close attention to the way that the scenography of *Blasted* forces the audience to surrender its distance from the material being witnessed. For example, Elizabeth Sakellaridou observes that in collapsing the geographical barrier between Leeds and a Bosnian battlefield, Kane refused a 'clear line between the "here" and the "there"', and thus 'devises an effective non-realistic strategy which disarms her British audience, removing any rational argument for non-involvement' (1999: 47). The collapsing of boundaries has been identified by a number of commentators as a key theme in *Blasted*. It is this strategy that provides a key to understanding audience experience of the play, as the remainder of this section considers.

Embodied feelings

Blasted has an overriding preoccupation with the perceptual realms of the body – its sensory capacities of smell, touch, sight, hearing and taste. This is emphasized by its setting: an *en suite* room brings into close proximity 'sleeping, eating, relaxing, cleansing and bodily waste, whilst, at the same time, providing a distinct zoning of bodily function and thus a more startling context for its conflation' (Iball, 2005: 324). Indeed, central to *Blasted*'s 'intended audacity is the displacement of Ian's abjection from the privacy of the *en suite* area to the middle of the bedroom and thus to the centre of the stage' (Iball, 2005: 324) – an action given ironic presage in his opening line 'I've shat in better places than this'. Christopher Wixson suggests that Kane deploys bodies in pain and pleasure as a way of disrupting the conventional languages of theatre – and he suggests that embodiment is partnered by the play's spatial disruptions (2005: 83).

In line with a number of other commentators (e.g. Aston, 2003; Rabey, 2003; Singer, 2004), Wixson uses Elaine Scarry's book *The Body in Pain* to underpin his analysis. He draws upon Scarry to express the connection between body and space in terms of the 'invisible geography' (1985: 3) of pain, as its full expression is beyond the capacity of words to communicate. The body in pain shifts to a place that is beyond another's reach and renders the sufferer helpless and stranded within it. Ian's damaged body and the wrecked room become merged in the image of his blinded face protruding from the floorboards. The audience know that these experiences are representations rather than actual experiences and yet, as Carney argues, *Blasted* brings together 'signs and experience' to express tragedy in a way 'which is a meaning only because it is a feeling, and an emotional experience only because it signifies' (2005: 280). Carney's main assertion is that rather than being reliant upon the shock effect that preoccupied initial media coverage and the first critical commentaries on Kane – considered earlier in this section in terms of the interpretation of the 'experiential' as 'in-yer-face' – in fact 'the violence in *Blasted* is profoundly aestheticized' (2005: 276) and the audience experience an emotional response to striking theatrical images.

As the next chapter considers, such a realignment of opinion on the perceived impulses of the play runs in parallel with approaches to production. This similarity is very interesting, as it suggests a shared response to the socio-political climate post-9/11 that prompts a particular view of the potential efficacy of Kane's play. As discussed, the playwright's assertion that 'the form is the meaning' (Sierz, 2001a: 98) has come to be equated with the potential to facilitate an ethical theatre. As further evidence of this critical accord, it is notable that the commentator Steve Waters has followed a similar trajectory to Urban (2001) and Carney (2005) in conceiving of 'the terror aesthetic' by which Kane short-circuits audience expectations. Waters suggests that 'the play has an inner didacticism which resides precisely in its refusal to tell and its compulsion to show' (2006: 379). Clearly, such a strategy relies on the visual dimension of the *mise-en-scène* for its realization. Thus, as the next chapter considers key points in the production history of *Blasted*, it takes a particular focus upon approaches to the scenographic, and proposes that this production element may, indeed, have provided kindling to fuel the controversy that the play first inspired.

3   Production History

This chapter is a brief history of the productions of *Blasted*. It considers the original Royal Court production in 1995 and looks at important revivals, focusing on the British stage. The chapter is arranged thematically in order to identify the key challenges the play poses for directors and designers, and to draw their approaches into comparison.

Play-scripts compel performances that are, effectively, larger than their own constituent parts yet, paradoxically, each performance is a limitation. There can be no ideal performance that captures all possible meanings and yet, to quote Jonathan Miller, by 'submitting itself to the possibility of successive recreation', 'the play passes through the development that is its birthright'. Miller describes these subsequent performances as 'afterlife', which he defines as a time when 'meanings that were not evident in the original production' are discovered. 'Afterlife' is a label that he finds useful because 'it draws attention to the peculiar transformation undergone by works of art that outlive the time in which they were made' (Miller, 1986: 23). A very particular combination of personal and political circumstances accelerated *Blasted* into its 'afterlife' at unprecedented speed.

At the time it was first performed, *Blasted* was held hostage by circumstances. The play became obscured by its realization, and opinion about *Blasted* was coloured by the accusations of gratuitous violence levelled by some of the theatre critics who attended the press night. As its perceived radicalism became assimilated, subsequent performances of *Blasted* began to produce not only meanings that were not evident in the original production, but also meanings that were overshadowed by the press. Furthermore, observation of recent productions, such as this study describes, suggests that the explosion of English realism might no longer be regarded as such an important aspect of the play, partly in response to shifts in the international political climate.

Thomas Ostermeier, director of the Berlin Schaubühne theatre, asserts that 'the startling thing about _Blasted_ is that it makes more sense now than when it was first staged ten years ago' because 'it is about something we currently understand: the fear that, at any moment, our whole society may be ripped apart' (Billington, 2005). This perception is, according to the British theatre critic, Michael Billington, typical of the 'specific European worship of Kane' (2005). _Blasted_ has become a landmark of both British and European theatre, having made a particular impact in Germany. In terms that make it clear that perceptions of a text's importance are culturally contingent, it is worth noting that German theatre was interested in _Blasted_ as narrative antidote to the over-abstraction favoured by German playwrights. It was, however, uncomfortable with the realist first half of the play – Germany having long abandoned that form. Conversely, British producers tired of realism were attracted by its disruption of those conventions, while UK theatre critics struggled with the stylized abstraction of the second half. So while in Germany _Blasted_ has become recognized as a 'modern classic' (Ostermeier, 2006a) and the debate is whether Kane is 'a good or a _very_ good' writer, in Britain the niggling question persists '_is_ she a good writer?' (Hillje, 2006; emphasis mine). It seems clear that British journalists and academics initially rendered _Blasted_ disproportionately important, according it landmark status – through praise and vilification – rather prematurely. To a significant extent, theatre historians seized upon the condemnations by the press as indicators of achievement. Elevating Kane to the giddy heights of 'revolutionizing theatre' proved to set advocates of that mythology up for a fall. As, for example, with Graham Saunders, who felt it necessary to acknowledge that 'the mortar bomb . . . was retrospectively more like a firework let off in a milk bottle – confined largely within the parameters of the play itself' (2003: 109).

It is evident that *Blasted* has been re-evaluated more rapidly than most cultural artefacts. Reappraisal, initiated in part by productions of other Kane plays, distinguished the play from the glare of its initial publicity. So, to an extent, the first phase of its 'afterlife' was about excavating the play from the scandal that obscured it. The trajectory of its reception was affected significantly by the playwright's suicide in 1999 at the age of twenty-eight, a period of 'afterlife' which has been recognized as polarizing the reading of Kane's plays, tending to either bracket her suicide as irrelevant to her art, or else seen to inform the approach to it. By 2001, a Sarah Kane season at the Royal Court presented an opportunity for the plays to be seen by a wider audience, allowing a focus on production rather than the hearsay of scandal, though the myth of the tragic and notorious artist is persistent: the story of Sarah Kane has 'opened up a wound in the theatre that has yet to be healed' (Waters, 2006: 371). The newspaper critic, Michael Billington, seeking to backtrack on his originally blind attack on the play, acknowledged that the play he had dismissed as 'naïve tosh' (1995) was in fact 'a humane, impassioned dramatic testament' (2001), while scholarship began to contextualize and question the limits of premature canonization (Morris, 2000; Urban, 2001; Sierz, 2001b; Luckhurst, 2002; Saunders, 2003; Iball, 2005).

As subsequent performances of a play proliferate, there is a dissipation of the assumed authority of its premiere. In the case of *Blasted*, this has been a particular and challenging shift because such a high profile was accorded to the two Royal Court productions (1995 and 2001). The Court's track record for angry young dramatists and the very public scandal at the Theatre Upstairs premiere combined with the close working relationship between Kane and James Macdonald (who directed both productions) created an umbilical link between play, director and venue. This link was consolidated by – and partly responsible for – the absence of _Blasted_ in professional production at any London theatre from the 2001 Royal Court revival until the visit of the Berlin Schaubühne theatre to the Barbican with _Zerbombt_ (_Blasted_) in November 2006. Straddling this event, Graeae Theatre toured the UK in spring 2006 with their production of _Blasted_, which then played London dates at the Soho Theatre in January 2007.

These months were landmark moments in the 'afterlife' of the play, especially as the proximity in their timing prompted comparison between the two productions (e. g. Quirke, 2007). Not only were ties loosened between the Royal Court and Kane but certain assumptions and prejudices were punctured. Graeae's production premiered in Tunbridge Wells. This somewhat confounded the opinion of Kane's agent, who had once said _Blasted_ would be 'quite difficult to produce in the regions' given that 'one has to be quite ruthless with oneself about who her audience actually was and how finite the numbers were' (Saunders, 2002: 144).

Meanwhile, Thomas Ostermeier's production at the Barbican expressed the 'afterlife' of _Blasted_ as European drama. It opened in March 2005 in Berlin, and London audiences witnessed a translation-of-a-translation, performed in German with English language subtitles scrolling across digital ticker-tape displays. Ostermeier has been Artistic Director of Berlin's Schaubühne theatre since 1999 and all five of Kane's plays are in the current repertoire of his theatre. This gives her work a larger presence in the Schaubühne repertoire (of twenty or so plays) than that devoted to any other playwright. Ostermeier recognizes Kane as a 'modern classic' in Germany, because her work is 'taken as a reference point' to the extent that 'young directors and actors all want to do her plays, and will do so during their lifetimes' (2006a). His interest in new British playwrights began in the mid-late 1990s when, directing at the Baracke studio theatre in Berlin, he staged several 'in-yer-face' plays (known in German as 'blood-and-sperm'), including Mark Ravenhill's *Shopping and Fucking* (1996). Ostermeier looked to these plays for a 'transfusion' of life into a German theatre that he felt was not speaking to his generation 'with the same intensity as rock music' (2006a).

With its accompanying Sarah Kane symposium bringing British and German practitioners into discussion, the programming of *Zerbombt* into the 2006 Barbican season seemed to acknowledge the 'staggering disparity of perception' noted a year earlier by Michael Billington. He contrasted Britain – where 'Sarah Kane has become a strangely marginal figure' and performances of her plays 'are startlingly rare' – with 'the rest of Europe', where 'Kane is widely regarded as the most significant dramatist to have emerged from any source in the past decade' (2005). Billington's assertion seems somewhat misleading. Its underlying implication is that all significant new plays are revived frequently in the UK. As the playwright Timberlake Wertenbaker laments, this is not often the case: the plays that are published in her second volume would all 'have benefited from second productions – some just to be seen by a wider audience. In the present climate, this is almost impossible' (Wertenbaker, 2002: ix).

However, as mythology to add to the Kane collection, the neglect of her work on the British stage is an attractive proposition: exalting her as undervalued can be gratifying to aficionados as it provides a paradoxical means of increasing her status. It echoes the oft-cited paradox of the Royal Court premiere, which, due to its short run, was attended by fewer than a thousand people 'making it perhaps the least seen and most talked-about play in recent memory' (Macdonald, 1999). Furthermore, productions beyond the UK were confined almost entirely to German theatres before 2001, suggesting that the production in the Royal Court Downstairs was catalyst to an international array of *Blasted*'s from 2002 onwards. There have been seasons dedicated to Kane's dramatic canon in Madrid (2002) and at the Schaubühne, Berlin (2005); European productions of *Blasted* in Hamburg (1996), Düsseldorf (1997), Milan (2002), Finland (Helsinki, 2004), France (Paris, 2005 and 2006), Greece (Thessaloniki, 2005) and Norway (Bergen, 2005). The play has been staged in Australia (Brisbane, 2001 and Sydney, 2003), Canada (Montreal, 2002), New Zealand (Auckland, 2003), Mexico (2002), South Africa (Johannesburg, 2002), North America (Seattle, 2004 and Los Angeles, 2004), Korea (Seoul, 2005) and Brazil (2004). British productions include Glasgow Citizens Theatre (2002), The Questors Theatre (London, 2004), Progress Theatre (Reading UK, 2006), Theatre North (Settle, Yorkshire, 2006 and UK tour 2007) and Graeae (UK tour 2006 and Soho Theatre, London 2007); there have also been many university productions.

Scenography: exploding the hotel room

The conditions surrounding the premiere of *Blasted* are complicated by the fact that its reputation became situated largely outside of the auditorium – initially while the media outrage was fresh, and subsequently because notoriety often proves irresistible to reviewers and commentators. Indeed, such reactions to the premiere have caused practitioners to be more than ordinarily aware – and sometimes cautious – of how the play might, and ought to be, received. It is important that the mythology is not widely accepted without investigating its causes.

The playwright Edward Bond compared staging the premiere of *Blasted* in the tiny Theatre Upstairs to 'hiding the Alps under the bed' (Logan, 2001). Seven years later in March 2002, Kenny Miller, director-designer of the Glasgow Citizens production, used the cramped Circle Studio to provoke a response from its audience 'as if they too had become trapped inside the hotel room along with Ian and Cate' (Saunders, 2003: 102). The scenography was crucial: 'for the first half the audience sit around the edges of that black, mirrored space – a vivid, queasily inclusive piece of set engineering', 'then the sky falls down, the roof caves in' (Phelan, 2002). Robert Dawson Scott, critic for the *Times*, describes how the audience were literally jumping out of their seats when the roof blew off (Scott, 2002). By means of contrast, in moving *Blasted* to the larger main stage, the 2001 Royal Court production accentuated what Ken Urban described as its 'epic exploration of the social structures of violence' (Urban, 2001).

In terms of patterns to be found in the 'afterlife' of the play, directors have paid close attention to the character relationships, as a means of re-framing the violent and explicit episodes. This is a consequence of awareness about initial accusations of gratuitousness as well as a realization of inherent qualities of the scripting. Miller stressed his main interest was in the relationship between the two characters – which itself raises the question of caution in response to notoriety, as an unnamed reviewer in the *Herald* suggested (5 March 2002). Miller's production communicated the sense of 'a completely new form . . . a political theatre worked through personal experience in a way which had not been seen even in the works of Kane's heroes Beckett and Pinter' (Brown, 2002).

In Ostermeier's Berlin staging rather ostentatious use was made of a revolve, which is becoming something of a directorial trademark as one was also used in his version of Ibsen's *Doll's House*. The stage spins constantly after the blast. But a revolve also disrupts the box-set in the first half, spinning the part of the stage with the bed on it around so that the audience witness Ian in the bathroom. This is a strategy intended to deprive Ian of his sanctuary; Ostermeier described in interview how 'Ian hides in the bathroom' from Cate who is 'the object of his perversion' (2006c). Ostermeier asserts that Cate's main motivation in going to the hotel is her desire to 'help' Ian, given that she knows he is dying (2006c). However, because the production shows Cate as very much the victim, sight gets lost of what Ostermeier stated as his overriding fascination with the play – namely that it expressed the complexities of all relationships, and how 'each and every relationship is to do with power': 'what impressed me was the love-hate, sad, horrible, tragic relationship between Ian and Cate, both of them looking for something else. The emotional rather than the socio-political was the draw' (2006a). Ostermeier situates himself in relation to the play as 'telling something which I have felt but couldn't express myself and Sarah Kane did' (2006b).

Even before the revival during the Court's Kane season, a similar attitude is evident from the critical reassessment of Kane's drama, as reviewers of her later works reflected upon the earlier, more physically brutal plays and observed love as their shared concern (see Waters, 2006: 372). This recognition informed a revised climate of opinion about *Blasted* (e.g. see Talbert in Saunders, 2002: 135), though the change was most pronounced in the expression of empathy:

> Five years ago I was rudely dismissive of Sarah Kane's *Blasted*. Yet watching its revival last night I was overcome by its sombre power. So what has changed? The space, the design, the lighting, the cast and James Macdonald's production are all radically different. But, above all, one sees the play through the perspective of Kane's tragically short career and her obsession with love's survival in a monstrously cruel world. (Billington, 2001)

Meanwhile, the Royal Court's team and associates had acknowledged that their production was, in part, culpable for creating the material conditions for misunderstanding. While, in the aftermath of the premiere, the Court's Artistic Director, Stephen Daldry, bemoaned 'one of our disappointments is that the metaphorical landscape has not been understood, or has been obscured by the controversy' (Bayley, 1995), the play's director, James Macdonald, acknowledged 'I think it's fair to say that there were images in the [first] production of *Blasted* that were compromised by the limitations of the Theatre Upstairs, both financial and spatial' (Saunders, 2002: 126). As Mel Kenyon observed the fact that 'on the Press night critics didn't get the play from the outset' was not entirely their fault because

> the set was not how Sarah had envisaged it. It was supposed to be one of the most opulent hotel rooms in the world and it actually looked like a bed-sit the result being that Ian's first line, 'I've shat in better places than this', which should immediately set up the play's black sense of humour and the ironic counterpoint between what you see and what you hear, simply didn't work. (Saunders, 2002: 147)

Indeed, James Macdonald pondered that 'for the audience, the most provocative thing might very well be to do a completely detailed and realistic production' (Saunders, 2002: 123). However, as reviews of international productions testify, any less than a full and thus convincing realization of a hotel room of the kind that is '*so expensive it could be anywhere in the world*' (1: 3) runs the risk of detracting from audience experience. As, for example, in the case of the Rude Guerrilla production in Los Angeles (2004) from director-designer Dave Barton, which one newspaper critic described as 'set in a supposedly posh hotel room in Leeds (crudely realised by Barton)' (Martinez, 2004). What should not be forgotten is that similar limitations applied to the premiere. There is a certain irony in Kane's claim that she pictured exploding the scenic conventions of which certain London theatres were so fond (Saunders, 2002: 41), and yet her play was staged under constraints that denied the realization of those conventions. The usual investment for a first play by a new writer was insufficient to meet the scenic demands that were fundamental to the text. The 2001 Royal Court production was the opportunity for *Blasted* to be seen by a wider audience, on a more convincing box-set, and for the making of amends for initial disservices done to the script. The exploding of this hotel room was important to the extent that it created the opportunity for a subsequent shift in scenographic priorities.

For the opening stage direction to be realized in its most literal sense, producing *Blasted* is expensive and high-maintenance. This is turn raises the (hypothetical) question of which is the lesser sacrilege to the text: a hotel room set that does not meet exacting standards because of budgetary constraints, or a design that does not aim for verisimilitude and yet, by different means, expresses the 'ironic counterpoint between what you see and what you hear' as described by Kenyon (Saunders, 2002: 147). Through comparative study it is clear that what appear to be crucial aspects have been reprioritized. The production history of *Blasted* is characterized by significant perceptual shifts, influenced by a changing political climate, and by approaches informed by various dramaturgical perspectives. From their accumulation, the complexity of the play is thrown into relief. Insights are to be discovered in comparing the contemporaneous Ostermeier and Graeae productions.

Ostermeier's 'dazzling production' (Billington, 2005) with its 'technically extraordinary' design by Jan Pappelbaum, created a setting that was 'significantly classier than any of the hotel rooms depicted to date in British versions of *Blasted*' (Halliburton, 2006). This caused a number of reviewers to complain of feeling distanced: the very expensive aesthetic was like 'watching a brutal but beautifully made film through highly polished glass' (Marlowe, 2006). There is a short history of comparable complaints, notably the 2000 Paris production which Edward Bond found distancing because it was too stylish (Saunders, 2004: 102–3), while Saunders expresses a similar reaction to the Kenny Miller production

(Saunders, 2004: 104). The issue of distancing also warrants attention in relation to the Graeae aesthetic, although this is not because of a glamorous stage design. Indeed, its minimalism evoked the early version of *Blasted* at the University of Birmingham in July 1993. Kane's agent Mel Kenyon describes how the set in this production was little more than a bed with a pink coverlet, yet nonetheless the experience was incredibly powerful (Kenyon, 2006). Rather, when the accusation of distance is levelled at Graeae – as a number of members of the audience suggested in conversation with me after the performance at the Stephen Joseph Theatre, Scarborough – it arises from a production that made a self-conscious decision to leave a lot to the imagination.

Graeae is 'Britain's foremost theatre company of people with physical and sensory impairments' (www.graeae.org). Jenny Sealey has been Artistic Director of the company since 1997, and co-directed the production of *Blasted* with Alex Bulmer. Sealey is deaf. Bulmer is blind. The production decisions developed from key contingencies: this was a touring production working to a limited budget; its performers have physical and sensory impairments; it aims for the broadest possible access for audiences.

The stage design for Graeae's *Blasted* was a simple floor, curving into an upstage lip upon which the actors could sit. There was a bed and a single red flower. In this manner, Graeae's pared down visual aesthetic was extended into the blast, presented by a video of a spinning ashtray projected onto the screen suspended as a backdrop to the playing space. Sealey describes how the ashtray was chosen as representative of the one thing that always seems to remain intact at a scene of devastation (Bulmer and Sealey, 2006). It was also evocative of Ian's self-destruction through his heavy smoking, and was coupled with falling petals in a visual echo of the shredded bouquet (here, a single flower). During the blast the mattress was thrown off, the bed tipped and the projection screens were thrown off kilter. Ian poked his head through the metal grid of the bed frame, which signified the grave under the floorboards. The Soldier was, appropriately, responsible for removing the pins that made the bed shift. The baby was made from gathering up the bed sheet. Though that was not the full picture: there was also a real baby in the arms of an actor-signer onscreen. The actor-signer paralleling Ian was at times smoking actual cigarettes and drinking from a real glass, while the one paralleling the Soldier was seen polishing his gun before the Soldier himself appeared onstage. Co-director Jenny Sealey comments, 'The actor-signers are fundamentally rooted in the characters onstage, giving witness to the "mind set" of the main protagonist in each scene' (2006b) and, fulfilling a dual function, almost as go-betweens, functioning as the 'ultimate voyeur' (Bulmer and Sealey, 2006). Also in shifting power dynamics: one of the best examples is when the male signer is replaced by a female signer during scenes between Ian and Cate (Bulmer and Sealey, 2006). They also enable the entrance of the Soldier to be presaged by his actor-signer, which David Toole described as an opportunity to watch and know Ian before his own entrance into the playing space – and for his entrance and immediate actions to be informed by that awareness (2006a).

For Graeae, actor-signers, description and transcription, all enhance the expression of the play's 'hellish challenge' to actors 'of inhabiting such complex brutal/vulnerable characters' (Sealey, 2006a) – and shifting power relationships, demanding that the audience collude in the acts of imagination that conjure the play. Indeed, actor-signers observe and comment on the action in the manner of a theatre audience. While the signers had real props, the actors onstage replaced props with gestures that expressed their physical absorption of things, especially Ian, who used mimic signs to indicate the inhalation of cigarette, the gulping and swallowing of mouthfuls of gin – as opposed to miming drinking from the glass or the act of smoking a cigarette. In this convention and in the speaking of character actions by the actors onstage as they performed those actions, there was a very particular immediacy that expressed the oft-concealed relation between thought and physical impulse. In a note to the director of the 1993 Birmingham production, Kane emphasized that the use of props was 'vital, even in a workshop production' (Saunders, 2002: 42). It is of huge significance that the Graeae aesthetic compelled the removal of the vast majority of props from the stage in a manner that drew attention to their importance. It is notable that a play whose first airings were held hostage by circumstance has found, in responding to issues of economic expediency and widening access, very effective variations in forms of expression.

'The stage directions function as lines . . .'

Speaking the stage directions becomes a way of realizing the most difficult structural elements of metaphor and landscape in *Blasted*. The seasonal variations in the rain heard between scenes pose a particular challenge. This is not a little ironic given that James Macdonald describes how the sound of seasonal rain was introduced in the blackouts to cover the sound of the scene changes. Kane had objected to the use of theatre music, and so the rain was a creative solution that mixed expediency with aesthetics (Saunders, 2002: 122).

The strategy encapsulates, even as it diverges from, Kane's intention and has been adopted by several subsequent performances. The first production to employ some spoken stage directions, broadcast over the auditorium's loudspeaker system, was also the first professional production to be staged in the UK beyond the Royal Court – seven years after the London premiere – at Glasgow Citizens Theatre in March 2002, directed and designed by Kenny Miller. As the *Guardian* put it 'now, for the first time, Scotland gets a chance to make up its own mind about a play that has become one of the most notorious of the last century' (Gardner, 2002).

Only one review mentions the convention adopted by Miller, and this is because the reviewer disliked the fact that the production's 'unflinching intensity' was 'unnecessarily defused by occasional stage directions read over the tannoy rather than shown' (Cooper, 2002). The 2005–6 Paris production of *Anéantis* (*Blasted*), by 'Sweet and Dycie' at venue MC93, Bobigny, Paris, and at Théâtre Darius Milhaud had a cast of four, with the stage directions played by Isabelle Chemoul. The director Stéphanie Correia described her reasoning behind this decision, recognizing the centrality of theatrical images, and perceiving Chemoul playing the stage directions as 'the witness of this history'. Correia's decision to describe to the audience everything down to 'the least details' (www.iainfisher.com) echoes Kane's scrupulous selection of each theatrical element in *Blasted* and, in the play's 'afterlife', offers the possibility that fidelity is possible through alternative means of expression.

In Graeae's production, the utilization of actor-signers onscreen is combined with the projection of the dialogue and stage directions being 'typed' onto the screen using a PowerPoint word-processing package: the script is staged across multiple media. This convention draws attention to the genesis of drama in the playwright's creation of the script – as does the voice heard over the loudspeakers, speaking those stage directions not spoken by the actors onstage. This voice is evocative of the voice of the playwright herself. Sealey described in interview how the opening section of the performance text felt incomplete until the company's subtitler, Claire Saddleton, suggested that the title of the play and the name of the playwright should appear on the screen (Bulmer and Sealey, 2006). The whole production foregrounded the creative process as a coming-into-being: the sense of emergence of performance from scripted blueprint. With a simultaneity that contributed to the palimpsest quality of the production, the subtitling invoked the playwright who had typed the scenarios playing out in her mind. Here was an 'afterlife' with the impression of birth.

Observing that all three characters in the play can be perceived as being disabled, Sealey recognized that 'placing disabled actors within the narrative allows a different interpretation of the play' (www.graeae.org) and thus:

> Directing a Graeae cast in a play in which so many metaphors surrounding disability exist will present unique challenges. We must ensure the actors own these metaphors. We believe the roles played by someone who is disabled will excavate so much more of Kane's language and that will emerge from a personal connection with the text. (www.iainfisher.com)

As Sealey discussed in an interview, the casting of Jenny Ellison – physically slight and unsteady when walking around the stage – challenged audience prejudices and assumptions about weakness that resonated in terms of gender as well as disability politics (Bulmer and Sealey, 2006). In the play, Ian remarks on her 'special needs' in terms of cognitive development, which seems to be based on the fact her brother has them rather than any evidence that Cate does (1: 5). This emphasized not only the play's critique of stereotyping but also the strength of Cate's choice to go out on the streets and sell herself for food. In production, Cate's childlike qualities included determination and defiance, and it was very clear that her part in the 'contract' to get food is more honest than Ian's supposed love for her. Equally, in terms of the uncompromising physicalization of the script, David Toole used his leg, a stump, for the rape of Ian.

Justifying gratuitous acts

I wrote [Blasted] to tell the truth. Of course, that's shocking. Take the glamour out of violence and it becomes utterly repulsive.

(Kane in Sierz, 2001b: 233)

One of the things most commonly known about *Blasted* before it is witnessed is that it contains offensive material. In attempting to shift the balance on this reputation, it can be tempting to detract attention from the play's explicit acts. In a description of Kenny Miller's production aesthetic for the 2002 Glasgow production, the newspaper critic Alan Chadwick observed 'surprisingly, what's most shocking about *Blasted* is how unshocking it actually is, particularly with the neutered sex scenes' (Chadwick, 2002). Another reason for avoidance tactics is that stage horrors can be very difficult to execute. The challenge of staging brutal acts convincingly is one of the things that a number of actors mention noticing about the play on first reading, with Kate Ashfield who played Cate in the first Royal Court production telling Graham Saunders that her first response was 'wondering how would these things work' (Saunders, 2002: 163). Similarly, the actor David Toole who was in the 2006 Graeae production comments:

> When I first read it I thought 'oh god, how are you going to do that' and it's going to be one of those crappy lychee in the pocket things [to represent an eyeball] . . . it's just such a nightmare to do . . . when we find out we weren't going to use the props, it was all in the description, we could really go for it . . . because when you're just saying it you can really emphasize these things . . . it's like eating the baby or sucking the eyes out, we only say it but because we're using the description you have to do it with an intent . . . it's got to be within that emotion that you're feeling at the time to make it real for whoever's listening to it. But then they can take it and make it whatever they want to make it. And it's like I say, that's when you find out who the real sick people are, because the ones who come up to you afterwards and go 'oh my god that was disgusting', I go 'well I only said he sucks his eye out you've made it what you want it to be'. (2006b)

Productions of the play in its 'afterlife' have exercised restraint in their staging, an avoidance tactic maybe and one that suggests maturity in the text and its producers. Immediately subsequent to the London premiere, *Blasted* was staged in Hamburg (1996) where, as translator Nils Tabert comments, it was 'easier' for the press to formulate a response because 'they knew about the reactions to *Blasted* in Britain' (Saunders, 2002: 135). Furthermore, the Hamburg production had also primed its reviewers by holding a press conference with Kane before the opening, and by sending them copies of the script a week in advance. Tabert observes that the intention was to make sure 'that it wasn't the scandalous nature of *Blasted* which would be the centre of attention' (Saunders, 2002: 135). Within the production, however, those elements of the text most likely to be received as scandalous had been approached with a relish that, to Kane's frustration, she found comparable to Quentin Tarantino movies (see Carney, 2005) – a strategy that Talbert describes as 'a glossy and trendy approach to violence' (Saunders, 2002: 138). Kane was troubled by on several occasions by interpretations of her work (see Stephenson and Langridge, 1997). In Hamburg, the audience were sitting around a realistic hotel room set, so that there were no hidden angles. Nils Talbert recalls:

> While I really admired them for how they did it, Sarah for understandable reasons thought it all wrong. It was too much 'in your face' – it lacked sensitivity, fragility and subtlety. It was more about the physical violence rather than the mental, emotional violence. (Saunders, 2002: 138)

In the Hamburg baby-eating scene, Talbert observes:

> He [Ian] really ate the meat which was absolutely terrifying ['chicken or something'] . . . you had this subtle sound of tiny

bones being broken which was horrible. But you know, even that
in Germany didn't cause a scandal, because most people are used
to German theatre being quite extreme. (Saunders, 2002: 138)

As a result of the initial outrage, British productions in particular
have approached *Blasted* with more caution. Finding a means of
justification is a frequent occurrence for directors approaching the
play. The most common is the assertion of relevance by citing
topical points of reference. The superimposition in *Blasted* of the
horrors of civil war upon Leeds has been lauded by some as prophetic (see Halliburton 2006; Waters, 2006: 373; Billington, 2005)
given the increasing threat of terror post-9/11 and the suicide
bombings on London transport in July 2005, a perception that is
encapsulated in some press reviews of the 2006 Graeae UK tour of
the play with direct reference to the experience of 'shock and awe'
(Fisher, 2006; Cooper, 2006). That *Blasted* was eventually viewed as
prophetic is somewhat ironic given that central to Kane's project
was to address British myopia.

In the 'afterlife' of *Blasted,* directors have observed the currency
of the play in a variety of ways. The least intrusive of these is
via directorial commentaries in programme notes or interviews. A
much more closed method was exemplified by the German director
Thomas Ostermeier. The connections that he highlighted to inter-
viewers in advance of the Barbican staging stressed the increasing
pertinence of *Blasted* commenting that 'what's most shocking about
the play' is that 'every day you perform it, it becomes more true'
(Halliburton, 2006). Ostermeier chose to focus audience attention
upon this quality by including a plasma television in the set that is
switched on intermittently by the characters during the first part of
the play. The audience cannot see the screen but they hear snatches
of newscasts making direct connections to Fallujah in Iraq and to
unrest among Muslims, which seemed to have 'emphasized Kane's

anti-war message' (Sierz, 2006) and was 'not mere factitious topical-
ity' (Billington, 2005).

During Kane's lifetime, a Belgian production directed by Yves
Bombay was shifted to focus on the baby due to the Dutroux
affair (Saunders, 2002: 67). The crimes of Marc Dutroux, a con-
victed paedophile and murderer, and the negligence of Belgian
police and government in dealing with his case, had provoked one
of the largest peacetime demonstrations since World War II, and
attracted international attention. Kane's response was that if
this had been the first production, she would probably have with-
drawn the play. Similarly, Ostermeier described in interview how
he was 'struck by how the relationship between Ian and Cate
echoes that between the Austrian Natascha Kampusch and her
kidnapper' (Halliburton, 2006). This was a current news item:
Natascha had escaped from a cellar after being held captive there by
an older man for eight years. The risk is that such specificity limits
readings, not least because it denies the audience capacity to make
connections for itself. For example, there were objections of
such over-specificity to the American accent of the Soldier in the
production by Theatre North (UK). A review of the 2004 Rude
Guerrilla production in Los Angeles makes it clear why such sign-
posting is not necessary, when it describes the performance given by
Ryan Harris (the Soldier) as drawing 'a hellish archetype with
unavoidable 9/11 and Abu Ghraib associations' (Nichols, 2004;
emphasis mine).

Afterlife relief

> *There is an honesty and a humour which permeates all my rehearsals*
> *because we are what we are and we work with what is possible and*
> *not what is not possible.*

> *(Sealey, 2006b)*

Jenny Sealey's description of Graeae's ethos answers very well the (hypothetical) question posed for this chapter: which is the lesser sacrilege to the text? A hotel room set that does not meet exacting standards because of budgetary constraints, or a design that does not aim for verisimilitude and yet, by different means, achieves its distinctive counterpoint. There are parities between some of the subsequent performances of *Blasted*, which, although stemming from varied requirements and constraints, appear to reach similar solutions integrating the various modes of theatrical signification to serve the thematic and metaphoric structure of the play. This renders the role of director-designer taken by both Jenny Sealey and Kenny Miller especially apt. On a number of occasions the dramaturgy has made a certain wilful mis-interpretation of Kane's instruction that 'the stage directions in brackets . . . function as lines' (2). While the academic Sarah Gorman notes there has been some reluctance towards innovation inherited from Kane's own dislike of interpretations of her work (2002: 36), sufficient critical distance seems to have been achieved that subsequent performances are relieved of the pressure to be so faithful. In the letter of the script they discover its spirit. The Graeae aesthetic in particular expresses the complex patterning of the text, and its implications, by overlaying the different elements of the *mise-en-scène*, realizing the manner in which Kane 'combines her linguistic spareness with an energy and an anger which feeds it' (Saunders, 2002: 145).

4 Workshopping the Play

This chapter offers a series of practical workshop exercises based on *Blasted*. It involves discussion of the play's characters, conflicts, key scenes, motifs and ideas, which groups of students can explore for themselves – along with suggestions for practical exercises for use by workshop facilitators. The content is also informed by new interviews with actors and directors who have been involved in professional productions of the play, by observation of workshops and by my own spectatorship and teaching.

The chapter addresses scenographic elements in parallel with the more often privileged domain of the actor/director; however, while it is important to recognize that *Blasted* is a very technically demanding play if the explosion of the set is done 'for real', logistical decisions are not a major concern of the proposed workshop. Rather, it is intended to facilitate a series of exercises that address the relatedness of central aspects such as time, place and characterization.

To this end, the main focus of the chapter is on bodies and space: particularly about discovering the ways the scripted lines and stage directions drive the physical action, which was central to the approach taken by Anthony Shrubshall, both in his teaching and in directing the play for the Questors Theatre, London (2004). He observes that spatial relations are a particular key to the play, because it is concerned with sex, violence and threat, and human behaviour in these terms situates its status and activity through physical proximity (Shrubshall, 2006). Thus in workshopping the play, a primary consideration needs to be how the text gets the actors moving around the room, and in contact with things and with each other.

It should be stressed that basic approaches to study and rehearsal are vital: a multitude of questions and possibilities arise from close reading and analysis; straightforward blocking of the play realizes relations between text and performance in terms of how the actors move around and utilize the set; and simply reading aloud key passages facilitates a powerful sense of the impact of the rhythms of the dialogue and inter-character relationships, tones and voices. When working through the script in rehearsals, simple exercises and discussion can be as revealing as more complex ones. As this description from my interview with David Toole, who played the Soldier in the Graeae production, reveals:

Everyday somebody would say something to you that would make you think differently about what you were saying . . . somebody would go 'I don't really see it like that' and you'd look at a line again and you'd go 'oh yeah, maybe it is that' and you'd say it differently . . . That was a good thing, because you didn't get stuck in your way of thinking . . . Even the first big speech that the Soldier has about going to the house, we tried that in all different ways. One that he was telling a joke to Ian, he was laughing while he was telling it, thought it was really hilarious that'd he'd done this . . . and that was alright, but it wasn't quite right. And then you'd try it as really threatening . . . but that wasn't right because that was too much of what he was saying, so we found a middle ground where it was almost neutral, like 'I went to the shop last week'. Saying those lines with that kind of attitude. And that just came from doing it different ways really . . . it wasn't that I'd decided it was going to be like that. We just kept trying and that was what we did for a lot of it because there isn't any black and white way of doing it, it's what made sense in the way those three people that did it . . . another three people would do it differently. (2006a)

Although these points regarding experimentation with level and intensity have a wide resonance, monologues are significantly sparse in *Blasted*, and thus workshop exercises paying detailed attention to the intonations of speech probably belong later in a process of investigation – particularly as Kane does not prioritize verbal communication over gesture. She does, however, recognize and exploit audience expectations arising from the conventional and constant flow of words in stage drama, and through those words, the provision of information and clarification.

The close analysis section in Chapter 2 considered the ways in which the scenic punctuation of *Blasted* is significant within itself: in the events that occur in blackout; in the punctuating darkness of the sequence depicting Ian's suffering; in related qualities of the play, such as Cate's fits which are personal 'blackouts'; in the stage directions that 'function as lines' (2); in Kane's use of silence; and of movement, gesture and action, in relation to the playing space and between the actors. Through the orchestration of *Blasted* its all-important image structure may be communicated effectively. And through this the metaphorical landscape is mapped. Many of these exercises select the opening scene as a starting point. The structures anticipated at the outset unfold through the playing time of the script, and its framework is established at the very outset. One reviewer captured the structure of *Blasted* very evocatively when he described it as displaying a 'grim logic' (Smith, 2001) and, as Saunders notes, the play has a unity of action that is achieved through stage properties (2002: 41).

Contextual considerations are also important, addressing the 'afterlife' (Miller, 1986) of the play and the ways in which current social and political contexts might inform production and reception.

In the current climate, the play seems immensely topical and makes a powerful comment upon international conflict. Yet it is also a response to and product of an observation of British society at a particular moment, as well as being prompted directly by Kane's reactions to events in Eastern Europe. The director James Macdonald describes how he did research on Bosnia (Saunders, 2002: 126) when rehearsing *Blasted*.

These exercises work towards a close understanding of the punctuation and layering of *Blasted*, exploring montage as a means of separating the various elements of production that are usually perceived as integrated in order to open up an interrogative space – and considering how this strategy is implied and anticipated within Kane's script. There is a subtlety and intricacy inherent in the play. Facilitating understanding and expression of the image threads and the latticework they form is crucial – particularly as, in the detailed awareness this develops, it becomes possible to accord more sophisticated contextualization of the list of atrocities pounced upon by the first press reviews and their tendency to simplify Ian and Cate into perpetrator and victim.

The world of the play

The room is the 'given': it is '*a very expensive hotel room . . . the kind that is so expensive it could be anywhere in the world*' (1: 3). Consider the opening stage directions very carefully, looking at Kane's list of contents, in order that you might begin to mark out the space. Be specific, and perhaps find some images of rooms like this. Discuss its material qualities and layout. You could make initial sketches and floorplans. How much space would there be? Where would the *en suite* be? How is the room equipped? And so on. Then think about two more points: (1) decide how particular you want to be about period: is this the 1990s or the present day? If the former, what would indicate that this room is an example of hotel décor in the mid-1990s? Research may be necessary to establish trends in interior design, colours schemes and so on (2) what aspects of the room does Kane prioritize and what does she exclude? The most obvious example of something you might expect to find and yet she does not mention is a television.

Walk through the opening sequence. Begin to map out paths around the room. This is the way that your initial decisions about the stage space can be tested and modified. An effective way to approach this task is reading aloud the opening stage directions and having participants mark out the walls, doors, window and furniture with tape. Two members of the group then move around the 'room' as Cate and Ian to explore the kinesics (movement in the space) and proxemics (relations between objects and bodies in the space) proposed by the script. The rest of the group sit where the audience would be, to observe and make suggestions. This exercise is initially about the flow of staging, not about characterization and the delivery of lines.

Develop this investigation by making specific proposals regarding the stage properties indicated in the opening of the play. For example, what kind of flowers is in the bouquet? What colour are the flowers? In approaching this design decision, chart the part the flowers play in the overall structure of images, listing the moments and their significance and resonance. The Schaubühne production chose white lilies – often associated with funerals and also with connotations of purity – while Graeae selected a single red rose and this production took the falling petals as its main motif, which was included in the publicity photographs.

The characters of the play: How they are introduced

Discuss what the exercises on the world of the play have begun to reveal about Cate and Ian. The director Anthony Shrubshall observes that 'Kane instils radically different energies within the two protagonists and this rhythmic difference is indicated in the stage directions for their entrance' (2006). How do the ways in which they inhabit the hotel room differ: which elements of the room do each prioritize? What does Cate/Ian see upon entering the room? What do these selections suggest about their character? Also what does Ian see when he looks at Cate, and vice versa? Each participant might close her or his eyes at this point and picture (and/or sketch) Ian and Cate in terms of physical appearance and dress. This is a good opportunity for pair work, in which these individual perceptions are compared and casting is discussed. Key information is to be found in the script. For example, how are the characters described in the stage directions? How do clothes function in the play? What do characters do/say in terms of their clothes? In her notes to the production team when the first part of the play was presented at Birmingham University, Kane described crucial elements of costume for Ian as tinted glasses and a tan leather jacket. She said of Cate: 'I'm not really sure but she looks boyish'. This vision of the characters might be compared with productions of the play through research into photographs of their casts and costuming.

All of the above tasks might now be applied to the entrance of the Soldier, giving insights not only into his character but also into Ian's in terms of the way his perception and habitation of the room are caused to shift. Even the design of the room has potential as a contributing factor in this dynamic, as my discussion with David Toole about the 'skateboard park' curve of the stage floor in the Graeae production reveals. David, born without legs, is a trained dancer and, in *Blasted*, he moved around the space supporting the weight of his torso on his arms:

> HELEN IBALL: What was so startling about your entrance – what was threatening – is the way that you move. You possessed the space, in a way that Ian doesn't. Which is really overpowering to

him. You know he thinks he does [possess the space] . . . but he doesn't. He needs his crutches: the gin and the cigs.

DAVID TOOLE: When we got the set, which was really early on, I think we got it about three days into rehearsal and the first time I saw it I wanted to play on it, and I think the other two didn't, which was good for the play in a way.

HELEN IBALL: Yes, that really worked.

DAVID TOOLE: Because Jenny [Ellison who played Cate] is unsteady anyway and on there she was struggling. And Gerard [McDermott who played Ian], I think he just likes his stages flat. And because I'm low down I loved it, it played to my strengths really. (2006a)

Next, it would be interesting to apply the above tasks to the two episodes in which Cate re-enters the space. Compare them with her earlier entrance and also compare Ian's reaction and attitude in each case. Then return to exploring the entrance of Cate and Ian and/or the entrance of the Soldier, but this time work in small groups. Extend the understanding achieved thus far by rehearsing these extracts of the text – informed by the completed exercises and by paying particular attention to movement and gesture. How do the three characters move differently? What are their habitual gestures? Thinking about these extracts in the context of the play as a whole, discuss what else is known about the characters' physicality and the ways they seek and/or find physical release. Consider how their personal anxieties and histories are focused on and through their bodies. How does this understanding affect the rehearsed extracts? Run through them again, adding the nuances discovered from these wider contexts. Also identify lines that seem to be key to each character. One of the most interesting aspects of Ian's character is his insecurity, particularly about how he is being perceived – and indeed judged – by others. His sensitivity to their remarks borders on paranoia, and for this reason he displays a tendency to be defensive. In thinking about approaches to performance during a workshop, it is also useful to consider possible responses from – and the impact of the role upon – actors undertaking the parts written by Kane.

For example, one aspect of Gerard's McDermott experience of returning to the role of Ian for Graeae's Soho Theatre performances of _Blasted_ was that he found ways of delivering the lines and shaping the character that procured more laughter from the audience than had been the case during the national tour. This desire for his character to be more likeable is an interesting one. As a character, Ian's veneer of confidence is thin and punctured easily: he is threatened particularly when first Cate and then the Soldier seem to be implying that he might be homosexual. Ian's heterosexual world view has been disturbed: his wife 'fucked off with a dyke' (1: 19). Gerard McDermott related this as a particular key to his character. Ian is anxious that Cate might harbour similar potential – certainly, her clothes suggest this to him (he thinks she dresses like a 'lesbos' [sic], 1: 19).

Ian's sexual identity centres almost entirely upon his penis: his need to ejaculate, his belief that his attributes are evidence enough of a 'manhood' that he characterizes as virile heterosexuality. This is the defence he uses when Cate asks whether he has ever had sex with a man (1: 19). He bases his social identity on the differentiation of sexual practices, and his profession as a tabloid journalist is shown to depend on these distinctions. Shrubshall describes how in the Questors production emphasis and attention were drawn to the contradictions and complexities in Ian's character through gesture (2006). He offers the flowers in an archetypal manner, hiding them behind his back before producing them with a flourish. He later does this with a cigarette, but this time the echoed gesture is ironic and cruel. This exercise might form a starting point from which to develop work with stage properties. You could look at the actions of different characters with the same props – the gun is perhaps the best example.

Run through the entrance of Ian and Cate/entrance of the Soldier again, taking the rhythms of the dialogue – extending these to include the subtleties of dialect as mentioned in Kane's character descriptions for more advanced workshopping – and particularly the silences as your focus. The director James Macdonald said that he learnt precision and the importance of punctuation from directing Kane's plays (Saunders, 2002: 126). Look closely at what is specified by the stage directions. Kane's agent Mel Kenyon describes the 'most extraordinary thing' about witnessing the Birmingham showcase:

> [T]hat first half of *Blasted* would not leave my head – the writing was exquisite, passionate, spare, raw, truthful and the relationship between Cate and Ian was extraordinary. Sarah's use of the space and silence was brilliant. In fact it was her use of silence that was the most extraordinary thing. (Saunders, 2002: 145)

The power dynamics in the play

Working in pairs – or perhaps more usefully in threes, with one member of the group as an 'outside eye' – and drawing on what you have discovered so far in the workshop, rehearse the opening unit of action and then rehearse the entrance of the Soldier. Cast the same actor as Ian in both while the actor who plays Cate also plays the Soldier. Discuss what these rehearsals reveal about the power dynamics by comparing your experience of the two scenes. Then switch roles, so that the actor who plays Cate/Soldier plays Ian and vice versa. What insights does this role-reversal give?

Read aloud the stage directions in the opening – ending with Ian's line 'I'm glad you've come. Didn't think you would' (1: 4) – first by the actor playing Ian, and then by the actor playing Cate, and then by a 'witness' figure – an actor playing the stage directions as done in the Paris production and described in the previous chapter. Discuss the effect these choices have on the power dynamics.

Experiment with swapping from female to male actors taking the role of the 'witness' at different points. Graeae played with scale and thus status/power because of the size of the screen displaying the video of the actor-signers. You could play with scale in terms of volume – the use of a chorus of 'witnesses' or the simultaneous presence of 'witnesses' supporting each character and speaking the stage directions. Explore the kinetic and proxemic possibilities of these actors in the playing space.

The exercise above is based on the one with which Graeae workshop facilitators began to get participants to work with the script in relation to the fundamentals of their production aesthetic. The workshop culminated by looking at the scene in which the Soldier rapes Ian. The Graeae exercises hold in common an interest in the connections between describing and voyeurism. Equally, they enable the complexities and ambiguities of the characters to be investigated and revealed – a recognition that shifts in nuance, in casting and so on will bring to the fore different elements of each character.

Working in groups of four, stage the rape scene between Ian and the Soldier. Cast it first with two male actors and then repeat with the physical score that you have rehearsed – but now the lines are spoken by two female actors while the rape scene is acted out in silence by the two male actors. Experiment with the physical positioning of the two female 'witnesses' in relation to the physical action. Repeat the exercise, replicating the staging but with the two female actors playing the roles of Ian and the Solider, while the two male actors speak the stage directions. Jenny Sealey described a workshop in which she asked the question 'which is worse, male rape or female rape?' (Bulmer and Sealey, 2006) which prompted without hesitation the response 'male rape'. The reason given was that male rape was perceived as more unusual, whereas female rape happened all the time – it prompted a shocked realization from the respondent and other participants of this particularly skewed perspective and what it revealed about discrimination in a society fuelled by the media.

Jenny Sealey describes *Blasted* as a play that forces performers and audiences to confront themselves with their own prejudices (Bulmer and Sealey, 2006). Look at newspaper articles that are reminiscent of what Ian says. The play draws attention to the importance placed by the media upon having a face-that-fits the story. Ian is dismissive of the Soldier who wants his story to be reported: 'I'm a home journalist, for Yorkshire. I don't cover foreign affairs' (3: 48). David Toole, playing the Soldier, described the key to his character as a hatred of journalists coupled with a painful recognition of how much he was relying on them to report his suffering (Toole, 2006b). The question of newsworthiness raises issues of an insidious and gender-biased form of censorship which ignores, as Kane's journalist says, 'soldiers screwing each other for a patch of land. It has to be . . . personal. Your girlfriend, she's a story. Soft and clean. Not you. Filthy, like the wogs' (3: 48).

Extended exercises with longer extracts of the play

This exercise was devised by a group of students I was working with at University College Scarborough (1996). The performance that they created used barely any setting but maintained vital stage properties. There was a square taped on the studio floor to indicate the walls of the hotel room, with interruptions designating the main/ bathroom doors. The bed was made from rostra. In staging the first scene, the students chose multiple casting for the character of Cate. The three young women looked, sounded and moved differently. The change-overs occurred during Cate's fits. It was a simple and effective technique in foregrounding the construction of identity and one of which I was reminded when a decade later I was sitting in the McCarthy auditorium of the Stephen Joseph Theatre, Scarborough, for my first viewing of Graeae's *Blasted*. The actor-signers appearing on screen (detailed in Chapter 3) served to bolster individual characters while simultaneously dispersing the illusion of singular real-ness and thus prompting the audience to remember the conventions at play.

Multiple casting of Cate also expressed her experience as being typical rather than an isolated case (of course multiple actors could also be used for Ian instead/as well). It also presented a range of body shapes and sizes and was a way of showing the audience prejudices and assumptions in relation to these. The approach of having other performers standing around the 'hotel room', which as I recall was a square marked on the floor in coloured tape, reminded the audience of the performance frame. This enabled actors (mostly women) to watch the onstage action – and for the audience to see their gaze. The exercise extends the strategy Kane employs in having Cate watch Ian as he writhes in agony as his damaged organs react against yet more gin (2: 24). Sean Carney notes that 'in contrast to the play's sense of privacy in reference to the character of Cate, *Blasted* ruthlessly exposes Ian in both a literal and a figurative sense' (2005: 283).

In the marked-out space, use group members receiving direction from the rest of the class to block the ends and beginnings of each scene in order to realize and thus discuss the shape and structure of the play and to begin to recognize the fundamentals of its image structure. Make a chart that lists succinctly the beginnings and endings of the scenes. Bridge the points on this list with what is implied to happen in the blackouts. Keep this list on display throughout your workshops. Split into groups. Make tableau for the beginning and ending of the scenes. Have one person in each group as a director/outside eye. This person will also be responsible for adding necessary description to the tableau, based on information given in the stage directions.

Create a list of what is not seen but implied in the play, that is, those events or actions that occur during its time-scale and environs and yet are hidden from view or that the script indicates are provided with cover in some way, for instance: during a blackout, when Ian or Cate is in the *en suite*, the scenarios outside the hotel. Create a parallel list of the means by which their significant absence is communicated – for example, sounds such as the following: knocking, running water or by symbolic use of stage effects and properties such as the blood seeping between Cate's legs, the hole in the hotel wall and the dust that is still falling, the shredded bouquet. This provides a way into looking at the metaphors communicated by key theatrical sounds and images. Small groups could select moments of text through which they might explore the gestures that are coupled with stage properties in order to add emphasis – for example, Ian's mode of presenting the flowers to Cate, or the Soldier's taking and eating Ian's bacon – and also how this implicates other senses, such as taste and smell – for the actors, but also possibly for the audience. Identifying key moments like this for each character, the exercises reverse the way Kane worked, as here the group are bringing together their individual perception of single encapsulating gestures towards a detailed description:

> I think there only three or four lines in the first draft that made it through to the final one. But that first draft stood me in good stead. I knew just about everything I could know about these characters. Having brought it all to the surface, the job of later drafts was to bury it again, make it felt rather than spoken. (1999b)

Ian and Cate are trapped in the remnants and repetitions of their relationship, which are condensed within the hotel room. This suggests the applicability of exercises such as those outlined above to excavate relations between memory and immediacy.

Working in smaller groups, or pairs, the class might then go on to workshop the staging of the episodes when Ian is alone in the hotel room – concentrating particularly on their punctuation by blackouts – and then move on to explore and/or discuss other violent and abject moments within the play, and the expression of experiences, such as pain, which are beyond words. To what extent does *Blasted* offend (and/or rely on offending) the audience? How are its means/intentions different in different sections of the text? How has the engagement it proposes for its audience shifted since the premiere? Have passing time, changes to the political climate, audience knowledge of the writer and so on, diminished the shock factor? How might productions need to adapt to these shifts?

In the light of this discussion, return to extracts you have already rehearsed and run them with modifications for different audience configurations and different sized auditoria. A further possibility that suggests itself is rooted in the sources that informed Kane, so that what is seen of Ian's body in the playing space – which is restricted already by his self-entombment in the baby's grave – might fuel workshop exercises reminiscent of Beckett's *Not I* (1972) where the performer's mouth is all that is seen. Hand-held torches would be effective for this exercise, and provide an interesting perspective, imposing limits on what the audience can see and the physical faculties available to the actor.

Another important and revealing series of exercises might reference socio-cultural contexts as well as the deeper implications of the dialogue. Look at the way Tennessee Williams uses the convention of the screen in his play *The Glass Menagerie* (1944). Thinking of images and captions is a good way of exploring the counterpoint between what is said and what is seen that Mel Kenyon observes is central to Kane's method in *Blasted* (Saunders, 2002: 147). It also echoes the strategies used by Graeae, where images and text that emerge directly from the play and are highlighted, and indeed transformed into theatrical metaphors, by the screening – for example, the spinning ashtray is a stage property that in being screened connotes the hotel blast as well as Ian's self-destruction. A computer running PowerPoint and a video projector makes such a project very manageable. It is an approach that can be extended for performance research projects, so that the contexts and influences shaping the play can be presented to an audience. For example, you could use lines from Bill Buford's *Among the Thugs* and images from the Sensation exhibition catalogue (1997) – perhaps the vulnerability of Ron Mueck's sculpted figures for the opening scene, shifting to grotesque mutilated figures by the Chapman brothers in the aftermath of the bomb.

5 Conclusion

This conclusion is a short but highly speculative account of possible future productions. When Sarah Kane announced that '*Blasted* now exists independently of me – as it should do' (1994: 51) perhaps it did not. As previous chapters observe, the 'afterlife' of the play is in overcoming and, at times, (over-) compensating for the hangovers caused by initial notoriety. Emerging out of this attitude, production and analysis appear to have matured to become increasingly self-reflexive and integrated. Graeae realized the possibilities of *Blasted* through an alternative dramaturgy. It was an approach that met Kane's demands for what fellow playwright David Greig calls 'an interventionist and radical approach from her directors . . . forcing them to go to the limits of their theatrical imagination' to discover 'poetic and expressionist solutions' (Kane, 2001: xiii).

Kane's agent Mel Kenyon states that 'only a woman could have written a play that understood violence so profoundly, from the perspectives of both victim and perpetrator without glamorizing it' (Thorpe, 2006). *Blasted* takes a marginalized perspective, one which recognizes the complex experience of young women, and which exposes masculinity to a particular kind of interrogation, while being brutally honest and even uncertain about the motivation of both positions. The play refuses us the comfort of simplistic interpretation from normative positions. Kane's work stages the complexities of socio-sexual relationships, infused with and often embittered by hierarchies that all too easily result in abuse.

In *Skin*, Billy notices 'an eight-year old mixed-race boy' who is staring in at the group of skinheads through the café window, he 'holds up his fist, showing the boy his swastika', the Boy 'bursts out laughing' and 'Billy gets up, furious' (Kane, 2001: 252–3). In *Gender Trouble* (1990), the academic Judith Butler described the process by which identity is constructed through punishment for getting the performance of gender codes wrong. Kane shows repeatedly that just because we seem to get the performance 'right' does not mean that it will be accepted without question or that the desired result will be achieved.

Through both form and content, *Blasted* recognizes the complexity of relationships and feelings, that every individual occupies multiple subject-positions and that 'class, race and gender divisions are symptomatic of societies based on violence or the threat of violence, not the cause' (Stephenson and Langridge, 1997: 134). Such a perspective might be harder to sustain in rehearsal. Director, Anthony Shrubshall felt by its absence the necessity of female presence in the studio, with the actor playing Cate the only woman in the majority of his rehearsals (Shrubshall, 2006). Both director Thomas Ostermeier (2006c) and the publicity for the Glasgow Citizens production in 2002 suggest 'pity' as an overriding motivation for Cate's decision to meet Ian at the hotel. The Citizen's flyer adds 'and naivety' to its brief description of her. It describes Ian as being there for his 'twisted version of love'. Graeae recognized something less binarized, and also granted Cate a more active sexuality – as do some of the reviews of the Glasgow Citizen's production (e.g. McMillan, 2002). Bringing Graeae's performers and production aesthetic to *Blasted* – and bringing with it women directors – destabilized elements such as shyness, coyness, pity, political correctness and the confines of male guilt, because it worked from the margins.

For future productions, there is a worthwhile blueprint to be discovered here. Kane's drama queered the pitch. The starting point is hands-on recognition that there are aspects of the play that deal with metaphors of difference, and the disabling impacts of society, at the same time as celebrating the contentious ambiguity within individual lives. All of this is empowering, particularly through its theatricality, of a kind which accords with Malgorzata Sugiera's demarcation: 'as a means of inducing an audience to watch themselves as subjects that perceive, acquire knowledge and partly create the objects of their cognition' (2004: 26).

Something else to be learnt from the 'afterlife' so far is that the risk of such strategies is distancing the audience. Annabelle Singer notes that Kane 'replaced realistic violence with figurative staging in *Cleansed*. By *Crave* there was no physical violence' (Singer, 2004: 166). This has also happened to *Blasted*, particularly in its British production history. This is a point which is implied too by the academic Graham Saunders when he identifies a cliché in relation to Kane's work – namely the 'sturm und drang' quality as tagged by Dromgoole (2000: 162) – and which Saunders disputes with reference to James Macdonald's productions, beginning with *Cleansed* in 1998: 'an approach was taken to uncover the ritual, imagery and symbolism that existed beneath its surface brutality'; Saunders notes that 'when given the opportunity to restage *Blasted* in 2001, 'Macdonald took care to accentuate its metaphysical qualities' (2003: 101) whereas Macdonald himself commented 'we did 1995 absolutely for real' (Logan, 2001). Saunders' comments are evocative of academic Christopher Innes, who observes the poetic quality of the work being obscured by suggested connections to the radical and shocking qualities of plays by Edward Bond and Howard Brenton. These observations are inclined to separate – or indeed, identify a ricocheting between – the poetic and the violent. This suggests a pattern ripe for change and raises the challenge to combine theatrical metaphor with shockingly convincing images.

Proposing even a partial return to what sounds suspiciously close to 'in-yer-face' demands that the (retro-) trendiness of violence is reconsidered. *Blasted* was under contract to the Royal Court at a time when Stephen Daldry was seeking to shift the predominantly middle-aged audience demographic in an attempt to re-invigorate his theatre, stating 'we have to listen to the kids' and working hard to create a 'cult of youth' (Urban, 2004: 357). In the new millennium, Kane's generation are fast approaching their forties. Today's young audiences – for whom Margaret Thatcher is a blurry historical figure – have been taught about citizenship in school and are conversant in political correctness. They are also becoming more accustomed to the threat of terror on Britain's streets. In its 'afterlife', assumptions about the audience demographic for *Blasted* will not serve practitioners well: as is clear from these observations from David Toole, who played the Soldier in Graeae's production:

> We started in Tunbridge Wells of all places and I was taking bets every night about how many people would walk out. And I think over three nights we had two people leave. It wasn't the mass exodus I'd been expecting and it was pretty good throughout the tour. And what I always found interesting was that it was older people that got more out of it in some ways. The older people know what war's like or relate more to the subject that's in there . . . maybe it shouldn't surprise us, maybe we're not giving the audience the credit they deserve. Students were a bit weird because they've studied the text and yet some of them are a bit immature about some of the stuff that goes on so you get laughs in bizarre places. Even when the baby got eaten at the end somebody burst out laughing. But that's what we were like in rehearsals though, we were laughing at stuff that we shouldn't. (2006a)

Given that time has passed, generational experiences are different, and although the play continues to act as a channel for fascination with Kane as an artistic tragic icon, the play also still functions on its own in its different historical moments, and something of its original context might serve well in the production of *Blasted*.

The *Sick* monologues address autobiographical and cultural-political contexts to enable the excavation of such detail, as does *Skin*. Kane conceived of *Blasted* in the early 1990s, drawing on the society she had witnessed while growing up in the 1980s. In the 2000s, Ian is even further out of his comfort zone. He is representative of a specific generation with his perception of football hooliganism, his experiences of a Britain distanced from world news and his confident misogyny and racism. This dates him. An elderly male actor, while keeping Cate at the age specified, might emphasize a wider generational rift and make their unsettling relationship all the more impossible to ignore. This is the ethics of the play and its realization is possible in what is called a post-feminist climate.

In one of the last interviews she gave before her suicide (Kane, 1998b), Kane expressed her exasperation about Cate: 'I mean what's she doing in that hotel room?' Kane puts Cate in the room recognizing impulses towards intimate contact with others that are borne of loneliness and longing and manifested in damaging habitual behaviours and skewed expectations. That she brings Cate back into the room at the end of the play shifts the perspective or, rather, pares down the impulses for contact until they represent interpersonal encounter at its most fundamental – the offer and acceptance of sustenance – in a scenario where the need is at its most intense. That is, after the worst has happened.

Timeline

Sarah Kane (1971–99)

This timeline focuses upon political and cultural events from Sarah Kane's formative years through to the Kane Season staged at the Royal Court Theatre in 2001, with emphasis on names and events this book identifies as having particular significance.

	Sarah Kane: Plays and Key Productions	Politics and Society	Culture
1977		Queen Elizabeth II Silver Jubilee	*God Save the Queen*, The Sex Pistols
1978			*Joy Division* formed

(Continued)

	Sarah Kane: Plays and Key Productions	Politics and Society	Culture
1979		Winter of Discontent (mass industrial unrest) Margaret Thatcher elected PM (Conservative), first female PM First heart transplant First test-tube baby	*Cloud Nine*, Caryl Churchill *Bent*, Martin Sherman *Amadeus*, Peter Shaffer *Apocalypse Now*, Francis Ford Coppola
1980		Outbreak of Iran-Iraq War 1st Maze prison hunger strike begins (IRA)	*Joy Division's*, Ian Curtis commits suicide *The Romans in Britain*, Howard Brenton (prosecuted by Mary Whitehouse) *Greek*, Steven Berkoff *Translations*, Brian Friel

1981	First reports of deaths from what later became known as HIV/AIDS	*Oresteia*, Aeschylus/Tony Harrison
	Riots in Brixton, Toxteth and Moss Side	
	(March) 2ⁿᵈ Maze prison hunger strike, begun by Bobby Sands. Sands is elected MP for Fermanagh and South Tyrone. The hunger strike ends (May) following ten deaths, including that of Sands	
1982	Falklands War	*Rita, Sue and Bob Too*, Andrea Dunbar
	(Apr.) Argentina invades the Falkland Islands	*Top Girls*, Caryl Churchill
	(Jun.) Port Stanley recaptured. Argentinean surrender	*The Real Thing*, Tom Stoppard
1983	American cruise missiles installed at Greenham Common, UK	*Victory*, Howard Barker
		West, Steven Berkoff
		Masterpieces, Sarah Daniels

(Continued)

	Sarah Kane: Plays and Key Productions	Politics and Society	Culture
1984		IRA bombing of Grand Hotel, Brighton (attempt to assassinate Thatcher Government) Football violence: Heysal Stadium, Brussels (–1985) UK Miners' Strike	*Rat in the Skull*, Ron Hutchinson *One for the Road*, Harold Pinter
1985		Greenpeace ship sunk by French agents in New Zealand Due to hooliganism, UK football teams banned from playing in Europe	*Les Misérables*, Trevor Nunn/John Caird *The Castle*, Howard Barker *Red Noses*, Peter Barnes *The Grace of Mary Traverse*, Timberlake Wertenbaker
1986		US and Commonwealth impose sanctions upon South Africa Chernobyl nuclear reactor disaster, USSR	*Road*, Jim Cartwright

1987	Iran attacks US tanker in Persian Gulf	*Serious Money*, Caryl Churchill
	General Election Conservatives re-elected	
	(Oct.) 'Black Monday' stock market crash	
	IRA bomb at Enniskillen kills 11	
1988	Clause 28 becomes Section 28 of Local Government Act (legislating against the promotion of homosexuality)	*Titus Andronicus*, Shakespeare/Deborah Warner
		The Secret Rapture, David Hare
		Our Country's Good, Timberlake Wertenbaker
1989	Fall of the Berlin Wall	Ayatollah Khomeini issues fatwa against Salman Rushdie, author of *The Satanic Verses*
	Tiananmen Square massacre	
	Tim Berners-Lee invents the World Wide Web	

(Continued)

	Sarah Kane: Plays and Key Productions	Politics and Society	Culture
1990		John Major (Conservative) replaces Thatcher as PM Trafalgar Square riot against Poll Tax Iraq invades Kuwait Reunification of Germany Nelson Mandela freed after 27 years in prison Lech Walesa becomes first President of Poland	*Racing Demon*, David Hare *Beside Herself*, Sarah Daniels *Mad Forest*, Caryl Churchill
1991	(and 1992) *Sick* trilogy of monologues (*Comic Monologue*, *Starved*, and *What She Said*) at Edinburgh Fringe	US air strike on Baghdad: Gulf War Croatia and Slovenia declare independence from former Yugoslavia Collapse of the Soviet Union	*Among the Thugs*, Bill Buford *Murmuring Judges*, David Hare *The Pitchfork Disney*, Philip Ridley

1992	Official end of Cold War Serbia and Croatia at war General Election Conservatives re-elected	*Mad*, dir. Jeremy Weller *An Inspector Calls*, Stephen Daldry dir. J. B. Priestley's play *Street of Crocodiles*, Theatre de Complicite *Angels in America*, Declan Donnellan and Nick Ormerod dir./des. Tony Kushner's play *Weldon Rising*, Phyllis Nagy *East from the Gantry*, Ed Thomas *The Fastest Clock in the Universe*, Philip Ridley
1993	*Blasted* showcased at Birmingham University (July)	Jamie Bulger murdered Serbian attacks on the Bosnian city of Srebrenica US attack Baghdad with British and French backing	*Trainspotting*, Irvine Welsh Hare trilogy: *Racing Demon*, *Murmuring* *Judges*, *The Absence of War*, dir. Richard Eyre *Machinal*, Stephen Daldry dir. Sophie Treadwell's play

(Continued)

	Sarah Kane: Plays and Key Productions	Politics and Society	Culture
1994		Tony Blair elected leader of Labour Party His slogan: 'New Labour, New Britain' IRA declare two-year ceasefire	*Ashes and Sand*, Judy Upton *The Striker*, Caryl Churchill *Some Voices*, Joe Penhall *The Three Lives of Lucie Cabrol*, Theatre de Complicite *Dealer's Choice*, Patrick Marber *Butterfly Kiss*, Phyllis Nagy
1995	*Blasted* premieres at Royal Court Theatre Upstairs, London dir. James Macdonald		*Mojo*, Jez Butterworth *Knives in Hens*, David Harrower *Disappeared* and *The Strip*, Phyllis Nagy *Pale Horse*, Joe Penhall *The Steward of Christendom*, Sebastian Barry *The Break of Day*, Timberlake Wertenbaker The Arts Council of England Awards the first capital grant from National Lottery Fund

1996	*Phaedra's Love* premieres at Gate Theatre, London dir. Kane Kane appointed Writer-in-Residence for Paines Plough *Blasted* in Hamburg	Manchester IRA bomb	*Trainspotting*, dir. Danny Boyle *Shopping and Fucking*, Mark Ravenhill *I Licked a Slag's Deodorant*, Jim Cartwright *Ashes to Ashes*, Harold Pinter *The Beauty Queen of Leenane*, Martin McDonagh *East is East*, Ayub Khan-Din *The Seven Streams of the River Ota*, Robert LePage
1997	*Skin* screened by Channel 4 television *Blasted* in Dusseldorf	Tony Blair elected Prime Minister Death of Princess Diana	Sensation exhibition, Saatchi Gallery, London *The Weir*, Conor McPherson *Closer*, Patrick Marber *Attempts on Her Life*, Martin Crimp *Blue Heart*, Caryl Churchill

(Continued)

	Sarah Kane: Plays and Key Productions	Politics and Society	Culture
1998	*Cleansed* premieres at Royal Court Theatre Downstairs, London dir. James Macdonald *Crave* premieres at Traverse Theatre, Edinburgh dir. Vicky Featherstone		*Via Dolorosa*, David Hare *The Blue Room*, Schnitzler/Hare *Never Land*, Phyllis Nagy *After Darwin*, Timberlake Wertenbaker
1999	Kane's suicide	New European Currency introduced NATO forces in Serbia Massacre in Kosovo	*Some Explicit Polaroids*, Mark Ravenhill
2000	*4.48 Psychosis* produced posthumously at the Royal Court Theatre, London dir. James Macdonald		*Far Away*, Caryl Churchill

| 2001 | Kane season at the Royal Court, including *Blasted* in Theatre Downstairs dir. James Macdonald
Blasted in Brisbane | 9/11 suicide bombers hijack planes and destroy Twin Towers, New York
US President George Bush declares 'war on terror'
GB joins US in Afghanistan war | *Credible Witness*, Timberlake Wertenbaker |

Further Reading

The play

Sarah Kane, *Complete Plays*, with an Introduction by David Greig. London: Methuen, 2001.

The playwright

Saunders, Graham, *'Love Me or Kill Me': Sarah Kane and the Theatre of Extremes*. Manchester: Manchester University Press, 2002. A detailed and carefully researched study of Kane's work and its contexts. Part one is organized chronologically and dedicates a chapter to each of Kane's plays. Part two consists of interviews with theatre professionals involved with Kane's plays.

Contexts and analysis

Aston, Elaine, *Feminist Views on the English Stage: Women Playwrights, 1990–2000*. Cambridge: Cambridge University Press, 2003, pp. 77–97. A carefully contextualized discussion of Kane as a playwright who rejected the idea of a being 'woman writer' and who was often framed as an 'honorary male'.

Buse, Peter, *Drama + Theory: Critical Approaches to Modern British Drama*. Manchester: Manchester University Press, 2001, pp. 172–90. The chapter on Kane takes a very particular focus, reading *Blasted* through the 'trauma theory' of Shoshana Felman.

Carney, Sean, 'The Tragedy of History in Sarah Kane's "*Blasted* "', *Theatre Survey,* 46 (2) (2005), 275–96. Carneys argues that rather than being a 'shock effect', in fact the violence in *Blasted* is profoundly aestheticized.

Dromgoole, Dominic, *The Full Room: An A–Z of Contemporary Playwriting*. London: Methuen, 2000, pp. 161–5. A personal, and indeed opinionated, account based on experience of working with Kane at the Bush Theatre, London.

Iball, Helen, 'Room Service: En Suite on the *Blasted* Frontline', *Contemporary Theatre Review*, 15 (3) (2005), 320–9. Locates *Blasted* in the contexts of its reception, before addressing the contingencies of its 'radical' *mise-en-scène.*

Innes, Christopher, *Modern British Drama: The Twentieth Century*. Cambridge: Cambridge University Press, 2002, pp. 528–37. Discusses Kane's work as poetic drama, primarily by identifying thematic connections among her plays.

Luckhurst, Mary, 'Infamy and Dying Young: Sarah Kane, 1971–1999', in M. Luckhurst and J. Moody (eds), *Theatre and Celebrity in Britain, 1660–2000*. Basingstoke and New York: Palgrave, 2005, pp.107–24.

Rabey, David Ian, *English Drama Since 1940*. Harlow: Pearson Education, 2003, pp. 204–8. A perceptive analysis that concentrates upon themes of physical explicitness.

Saunders, Graham, '"Just a Word on a Page and There Is the Drama." Sarah Kane's Theatrical Legacy', *Contemporary Theatre Review*, 13 (1) (2003), 97–110. Discussion of the divergent responses provoked by Kane's work, with reference to influences on Kane and consideration of production histories.

Saunders, Graham, '"Out Vile Jelly": Sarah Kane's *Blasted* and Shakespeare's *King Lear*', *New Theatre Quarterly*, 20(1) (2004), 69–78. Discusses the play's approaches to re-writing *King Lear* in terms of dialogue, theme, theatrical imagery, and tragic form.

Sellar, Tom, 'Truth and Dare: Sarah Kane's *Blasted*', *Theater*, 27 (1) (1996), 29–34. Surveys press responses to the premiere, drawing heavily upon parallels with reactions to Edward Bond's *Saved*.

Sierz, Aleks, '"The Element That Most Outrages": Morality, Censorship and Sarah Kane's *Blasted*', *European Studies*, 17 (2001), 225–39. Examines reactions to *Blasted* in relation to the shifting characteristics of censorship in post-war British theatre.

Sierz, Aleks, *In-Yer-Face Theatre: British Drama Today*. London: Faber, 2001. Identifies Kane as 'the quintessential in-yer-face writer of the decade' and contains a well-researched chapter discussing four of Kane's plays, with a section focusing on *Blasted*.

Singer, Annabelle, 'Don't Want to Be This: The Elusive Sarah Kane', *The Drama Review*, 48 (2) (2004), 139–71. Contrasts reactions to Kane's plays in relation to her depression and suicide.

Urban, Ken, 'An Ethics of Catastrophe: The Theatre of Sarah Kane', *Performing Arts Journal*, 69 (2001), 36–69. Discusses how Kane's drama altered the landscape of British theatre in the 1990s, using the 2001 season at the Royal Court as his point of reference.

Waters, Steve, 'Sarah Kane: From Terror to Trauma,' in Mary Luckhurst (ed.), *A Companion to Modern British and Irish Drama*. Oxford: Blackwell, 2006, pp. 371–82. Identifies phases in the reception of her work from reviewers – at the premiere and in terms of 'terror aesthetics'.

Wixson, Christopher, '"In Better Places": Space, Identity, and Alienation in Sarah Kane's *Blasted*', *Comparative Drama*, 39 (1) (2005), 75–91. Wixson argues that it was Kane's defiance of the rules of realism that infuriated her critics more than her play's shocking images.

Websites

www.iainfisher.com/kane.html Site dedicated to Kane's work. Contains an archive, links, information on forthcoming productions, and photographs.

www.inyerface-theatre.com Site maintained by Aleks Sierz which includes information on Kane and a wealth of other contemporary British dramatists.

References

Note: All references to *Blasted* and Kane's other plays are to *Sarah Kane: Complete Plays*, with an Introduction by David Greig. London: Methuen, 2001. All parenthetical references to the plays cite the scene number followed by the page number – for example (2: 34) refers to scene two, page thirty-four.

Alvarez, Al (1971), *The Savage God: A Study of Suicide*. London: Bloomsbury.

Armistead, Claire (1998), 'No Pain, No Kane'. *Guardian*, 29 April.

Aston, Elaine (2003), *Feminist Views on the English Stage: Women Playwrights, 1990–2000*. Cambridge: Cambridge University Press.

Aston, Elaine and Janelle Reinelt (eds.) (2001), *The Cambridge Companion to Modern British Women Playwrights*. Cambridge: Cambridge University Press.

Barker, Howard (1995), *Collected Plays: Volume Three*. London: John Calder.

Barker, Howard (1997 [1989]), *Arguments for a Theatre*. Manchester: Manchester University Press, 3rd edn.

Bayley, Clare (1995), 'A Very Angry Young Woman'. *Independent*, 23 January.

Benedict, David (1995), 'Disgusting Violence? Actually it's Quite a Peaceful Play'. *Independent on Sunday*, 23 January.

Berry, Kathleen S. (2000), *The Dramatic Arts and Cultural Studies: Acting Against the Grain*. New York: Falmer Press.

Billington, Michael (1995), Review of *Blasted*. *Guardian*, 20 January.

Billington, Michael (2001), Review of *Blasted*. *Guardian*, 5 April.

Billington, Michael (2005), 'The Best British Playwright You'll Never See'. *Guardian*, 23 March.

Bond, Edward (1977), *Plays: One*. London: Methuen.

Brenton, Howard (2002), 'Freedom in Chaos'. *Guardian*, 21 September.

Brown, Mark (2002), Preview of *Blasted*. *Scotland on Sunday*, 3 March.

Buford, Bill (1991), *Among the Thugs*. London: Arrow.

Bulmer, Alex and Jenny Sealey (2006), interview by Helen Iball, 24 October.

Buse, Peter (2001), *Drama + Theory: Critical Approaches to Modern British Drama*. Manchester: Manchester University Press.

Butler, Judith (1990), *Gender Trouble*. London: Routledge.

Cardinal, Roger (1984), *Expressionism*. London: Paladin Books.

Carney, Sean (2005), 'The Tragedy of History in Sarah Kane's *Blasted*', *Theatre Survey*, 46 (2), 275–96.

Cetinsky, Karol (1956), *The House of Dolls*. Toronto: Senate Books.

Chadwick, Alan (2002), Review of *Blasted*. *Metro*, 11 March.

Chambers, Colin (ed.) (2002), *The Continuum Companion to Twentieth Century Theatre*. London: Continuum.

Clapp, Susannah (1998), 'West End Girls (and Boys)'. *Observer*, 24 May.

Cooper, Neil (2002), Review of *Blasted*. *Herald*, 8 March.

Cooper, Neil (2006), Review of *Blasted*. *Herald*, 21 April.

Coveney, Michael (1995), 'Applause for Thought'. *Observer*, 31 December.

Crimp, Martin with Paul Godfrey, Meredith Oakes, and Gregory Motton (1995), Letter to the *Guardian*, 23 January.

De Marinis, Marco (1987), 'Dramaturgy of the Spectator'. *The Drama Review*, 31 (2), 100–14.

Diamond, Elin (1997), *Unmaking Mimesis: Essays on Feminism and Theatre*. London: Routledge.

Dromgoole, Dominic (2000), *The Full Room: An A–Z of Contemporary Playwriting*. London: Methuen.

Eagleton, Terry (2002), *Sweet Violence: The Idea of the Tragic*. Oxford: Blackwell.

Edgar, David (1999), *State of Play: Playwrights on Playwriting*. London: Faber.

Edgar, David (2005), 'Unsteady States: Theories of Contemporary New Writing'. *Contemporary Theatre Review*, 15 (3), 297–308.

Eldridge, David (2003), 'In-Yer-Face and After'. *Studies in Theatre and Performance* 23 (1), 55–8.

Ellison, Mike and Alex Bellos (1995), '*Blasted*: A Deeply Moral and Compassionate Piece of Theatre or Simply a Disgusting Feast of Filth?' *Guardian*, 20 January.

Fisher, Mark (2006), 'Shock and Awe in Blast from the Past'. *Scotland on Sunday*, 16 April.

Fleche, Anne (1997), *Mimetic Disillusion: Eugene O'Neill, Tennessee Williams, and U.S. Dramatic Realism*. Tuscaloosa and London: University of Alabama Press.

Gardner, Lyn (2002), Preview of *Blasted*. *Guardian*, 16 March.

Gardner, Lyn with James Macdonald, and Michael Billington (1999), 'Sarah Kane: Of Love and Outrage'. *Guardian* Obituaries, 23 February.

Garner, Stanton B., Jr (1994), *Bodied Spaces: Phenomenology and Performance in Contemporary Drama*. Ithaca, NY: Cornell University Press.

Gibbons, Fiachra (1999), 'Royal Court Takes on Kane's Last Play'. *Guardian*, 20 September.

Gorman, Sarah (2002), 'The Mythology of Sarah Kane: How to Avoid Reading *4.48 Psychosis* as a Suicide Note'. *Anglo Files*, 126, 35–42.

Gottlieb, Vera and Colin Chambers (eds.) (1999), *Theatre in a Cool Climate*. Oxford: Amber Lane Press.

Greig, David (2003), 'A Tyrant for All Time'. *Guardian*, 28 April.

Halliburton, Rachel (2006), 'Every Day it Becomes More True'. *Time Out*, 1–8 November.

Hattenstone, Simon (2000), 'A Sad Hurrah'. *Guardian* Weekend, 1 July.

Hillje, Jens (2006), Panel discussion chaired by Dan Rebellato, Sarah Kane Symposium. London Barbican, 11 November.

Hilton, Julian (ed.) (1993), *New Directions in Theatre*. London: Macmillan.

Iball, Helen (2005), 'Room Service: En Suite on the *Blasted* Frontline'. *Contemporary Theatre Review*, 15 (3), 320–9.

Innes, Christopher (2002), *Modern British Drama: The Twentieth Century*. Cambridge: Cambridge University Press.

Jenkins, Amy (2007), '1990s'. *Guardian* Weekend, 26 May.

Kane, Sarah (1994), Afterword to *Blasted* in Pamela Edwardes (ed.), *Frontline Intelligence: New Plays for the Nineties*. London: Methuen.

Kane, Sarah (1998a), Public interview by Dan Rebellato, 'Brief Encounter' Platform. Royal Holloway College, London, 3 November.

Kane, Sarah (1998b), Interview by Aleks Sierz, 14 September.

Kane, Sarah (1998c), 'Drama with Balls'. *Guardian*, 20 August.

Kane, Sarah (1998d), 'The Only Thing I Remember Is . . .'. *Guardian*, 13 August.

Kane, Sarah (1999a), Letter to Aleks Sierz, 4 February.

Kane, Sarah (1999b), Letter to Aleks Sierz, 18 January.

Kane, Sarah (2001), *Complete Plays*, with an Introduction by David Greig. London: Methuen.

Kenyon, Mel (2006), Panel discussion chaired by Dan Rebellato, Sarah Kane Symposium. London Barbican, 11 November.

Kingston, Jeremy (1995), 'Shocking Scenes in Sloane Square'. *Times*, 20 January.

Leahy, Terry (1994), 'Taking Up a Position: Discourses of Femininity and Adolescence in the Context of Man/Girl Relationships'. *Gender and Society*, 8 (1), 48–72.

Lehmann, Hans-Thies (2006 [1999]), *Postdramatic Theatre*. trans. Karen Jürs-Munby, London: Routledge.

Logan, Brian (2001), 'The Savage Mark of Kane'. *Independent on Sunday*, 1 April.

Luckhurst, Mary (2002), 'An Embarrassment of Riches: Women Dramatists in 1990s Britain', in Bernhard Reitz and Mark Berninger (eds.), *British Drama of the 1990s: Anglistik and Englischunterricht*. Heidelberg: University of Heidelberg, pp. 65–77.

Macdonald, James (1995), 'Blasting Back at the Critics'. *Observer* Review, 22 January.

Macdonald, James (1999), 'They Never Got Her'. *Observer*, 28 February.

Marlowe, Sam (2006), Review of *Zerbombt*, *Times*, 9 November.

Martinez, Julio (2004), '*Blasted* Exposes the Ugly Heart of War'. *U-Daily News*, 2 July.

Marwick, Andrew (2003), *British Society Since 1945*. London: Penguin.

McMillan, Joyce (2002), 'No Damage Limitations'. *Scotsman*, 13 March.

Megson, Chris (2004), '"The Spectacle Is Everywhere": Tracing the Situationist Legacy in British Playwrighting Since 1968'. *Contemporary Theatre Review*, 14 (2), 17–28.

Miller, Jonathan (1986), *Subsequent Performances*. London: Faber.

Morris, Peter (2000), 'The Brand of Kane'. *Arete*, 4, 142–52.

Nichols, David C. (2004), Review of *Blasted*. *LA Times*, 25 June.

Nightingale, Benedict (1998), *The Future of Theatre*. London: Phoenix.

Ostermeier, Thomas (2006a), Interview by Mark Ravenhill, Sarah Kane Symposium. London Barbican, 11 November.

Ostermeier, Thomas (2006b), Panel discussion chaired by Dan Rebellato, Sarah Kane Symposium. London Barbican, 11 November.

Ostermeier, Thomas (2006c), Interview by Helen Iball, 11 November.

Peacock, D. Keith (1999), *Thatcher's Theatre*. Westport, CT: Greenwood Press.

Peter, John (1995), 'Alive When Kicking'. *Sunday Times*, 29 January.

Phelan, Stephen (2002), 'The Horror, the Horror'. *Sunday Herald*, 10 March.

Quirke, Kieron (2007), 'Shocking but Brilliant'. *Evening Standard*, 19 January.

Rabey, David Ian (2003), *English Drama Since 1940*. Harlow: Pearson Education, 2003.

Ravenhill, Mark (2004), 'A Tear in the Fabric: The James Bulger Murder and New Theatre Writing in the "Nineties"'. *New Theatre Quarterly*, 20 (4), 305–14.

Ravenhill, Mark (2006), 'The Beauty of Brutality'. *Guardian* Review, 28 October.

Rebellato, Dan (1999), 'Sarah Kane: An Appreciation'. *New Theatre Quarterly*, 59, 280–1.

Ritchie, James M. (1968), *Seven Expressionist Plays*. London: Calder.

Rosenthal, Norman, et al. (1997), *Sensation: Young British Artists from the Saatchi Collection*. London: Royal Academy of Arts.

Sakellaridou, Elizabeth (1999), 'New Faces for British Political Theatre'. *Studies in Theatre and Performance*, 20 (1), 43–51.

Saunders, Graham (2002), *'Love Me or Kill Me': Sarah Kane and the Theatre of Extremes*. Manchester: Manchester University Press.

Saunders, Graham (2003), '"Just a Word on a Page and There Is the Drama." Sarah Kane's Theatrical Legacy'. *Contemporary Theatre Review*, 13 (1), 97–110.

Saunders, Graham (2004), '"Out Vile Jelly": Sarah Kane's *Blasted* and Shakespeare's *King Lear*'. *New Theatre Quarterly*, 20 (1), 69–78.

Scarry, Elaine (1985), *The Body in Pain: The Making and Unmaking of the World*. Oxford: Oxford University Press.

Schneider, Rebecca (1997), *The Explicit Body in Performance*. London: Routledge.

Scott, Robert Dawson (2002), Review of *Blasted*. *Times*, 10 March.

Sealey, Jenny (2006a), email to *Plymouth Evening Herald*, 4 April.

Sealey, Jenny (2006b), email to *Metro Liverpool*, 22 March.

Sellar, Tom (1996), 'Truth and Dare: Sarah Kane's *Blasted*'. *Theater*, 27 (1), 29–34.

Shrubshall, Anthony (2006), interview by Helen Iball, 3 November.

Sierz, Aleks (2001a), *In-Yer-Face Theatre: British Drama Today*. London: Faber.

Sierz, Aleks (2001b), '"The Element That Most Outrages": Morality, Censorship and Sarah Kane's *Blasted*'. *European Studies* 17, 225–39.

Sierz, Aleks (2001c), 'Raising Kane'. *What's On in London*, 28 March.

Sierz, Aleks (2003), 'Review of *Sarah Kane: Complete Plays*'. *Contemporary Theatre Review*, 13 (1), 115–7.

Sierz, Aleks (2004), 'Sarah Kane', in H. C. G. Matthew and B. Harrison (eds.), *Oxford Dictionary of National Biography*. Oxford: Oxford University Press, pp. 873–4.

Sierz, Aleks (2005), 'Beyond Timidity? The State of British New Writing'. *PAJ: A Journal of Performance and Art*, 27 (3), 55–61.

Sierz, Aleks (2006), '"For Us, She Is a Classic"'. *Telegraph*, 23 October.

Singer, Annabelle (2004), 'Don't Want to Be This: The Elusive Sarah Kane'. *The Drama Review*, 48 (2), 139–71.

Smith, Andrew (2001), 'The Violence of the Damned'. *Observer* Review, 8 April.

Spencer, Charles (2006), 'Blast from the Past Still Chills'. *Telegraph*, 9 November.

States, Bert O. (1985), *Great Reckonings in Little Rooms: On the Phenomenology of Theatre*. Berkeley: University of California Press.

Steiner, George (1961), *The Death of Tragedy*. London: Faber and Faber.

Stephenson, Heidi and Natasha Langridge (1997), *Rage and Reason: Women Playwrights on Playwriting*. London: Methuen.

Sugiera, Małgorzata (2004), 'Beyond Drama: Writing for Postdramatic Theatre'. *Theatre Research International*, 29 (1), 6–28.

Taylor, John Russell (1971), 'British Dramatists: The New Arrivals. The Dark Fantastic'. *Plays and Players*, 18, 24–7.

Thorpe, Adam (2006), 'Attack!' *Guardian*, 22 February.

Tinker, Jack (1995), 'This Disgusting Feast of Filth'. *Daily Mail*, 27 January.

Toole, David (2006a), Interview by Helen Iball, 28 June.

Toole, David (2006b), Interview by Helen Iball, 12 May.

Urban, Ken (2001), 'An Ethics of Catastrophe: The Theatre of Sarah Kane'. *Performing Arts Journal*, 69, 36–69.

Urban, Ken (2004), 'Towards a Theory of Cruel Britannia: Coolness, Cruelty, and the "Nineties"'. *New Theatre Quarterly*, 20 (4), 354–72.

Wandor, Michelene (2001), *Post-War British Drama: Looking Back in Gender*. London: Routledge.

Waters, Steve (2006), 'Sarah Kane: From Terror to Trauma,' in M. Luckhurst (ed.), *A Companion to Modern British and Irish Drama*. Oxford: Blackwell, pp. 371–82.

Wertenbaker, Timberlake (2002), *Plays: Two*. London: Faber.

Wixson, Christopher (2005), '"In Better Places": Space, Identity, and Alienation in Sarah Kane's *Blasted*'. *Comparative Drama*, 39 (1), 75–91.

Index